Remodeling
on the Money

15 | Innovative Projects
Designed to Add Value to Your Home

Alan J. Heavens

KAPLAN

PUBLISHING

New York

Editorial Director: Jennifer Farthing
Development Editor: Carolyn Hanson
Production Editor: Fred Urfer
Cover Designer: Carly Schnur

Published by Kaplan Publishing, a division of Kaplan, Inc.
1 Liberty Plaza, 24th floor
New York, NY 10006

Printed in the United States of America

September 2007
10 9 8 7 6 5 4 3 2 1

ISBN-13: 978-1-4277-5480-6

REMODELING ON THE MONEY

To my wife, Ellen Gray—
she still knows why.

Table of Contents

Acknowledgments

My thanks to Joanne McLaughlin, real estate and home and design editor of *The Philadelphia Inquirer*, for her support and for suggesting the title of this book. I am also deeply grateful to those who have shared their remodeling experiences for these pages. A special thanks also to Jay Cipriani, president of Cipriani Builders of Woodbury, New Jersey, for allowing me to bring my camera on some of the 100 remodeling jobs he completes each year, and to the students in my classes at the Temple University Real Estate Institute for allowing me try out my ideas on them and for their constructive criticism.

Preface

My first book, *What No One Ever Tells You About Renovating Your Home*, was what one writer described as a cautionary tale, designed to help you avoid many of the mistakes that I and others made in making changes, necessary and sometimes not so necessary, to our houses.

Remodeling on the Money, on the other hand, is a how-to book. How-to doesn't mean that once you are finished reading, you should run out to the home center, buy a reciprocating saw, and cut a hole in the side of your house for an addition. How-to, in this instance, means how certain remodeling projects should be done, what kinds of problems you'll likely face, and how you should approach them. This will mean, in most cases, hiring a qualified professional to do the job, selecting materials suitable for the work, and then writing a check.

What makes this book unusual is that once you buy it, it becomes your key to an evolving Internet portal that will provide you with all the information you will need to remodel on the money. The work and materials described in every chapter of this book will be demonstrated and illustrated on the website—in photographs, in videos that can be downloaded on an MP3 player and taken on-site, and in podcasts with professionals describing the work in detail. You will also find links to manufacturers and service providers where you can pick the right appliance, window, or door for your job, and where you can monitor continually changing prices of both materials and labor for your particular area.

Whether you have *Remodeling on the Money* in your hands or www.remodelingonthemoney.com on your computer screen, you will have access to the most comprehensive and up-to-date remodeling information available.

The most important ingredient in any remodeling job is the contractor, and that's why we'll address how to find and successfully work with one before we get deeply into the book. In *What No One Ever Tells You About Renovating Your Home*, in the chapter titled "The Perfect Match," we met Alex and Beth Cerrato, who were able to find and work with a contractor when they decided to build a two-story addition that virtually doubled the square footage of their house to accommodate them and their two young sons.

The Cerratos' contractor, Jay Cipriani, is not the typical remodeling contractor. He wowed the couple at their first meeting (they had interviewed four others; Jay was recommended by a neighbor). He was detail-oriented; he assured them without hesitation that they could have what they wanted, and even suggested trade-offs, such as forgoing the double Jacuzzi tub in the master bath in favor of the basement addition.

Jay also was honest with Beth and Alex—in Alex's words, "He told us it wouldn't be fast, easy, or cheap, but he said it could be done." Even before the contract was signed, Jay brought Alex and Beth to his office in the evening for two hours a week over 10 weeks for formal education on methods and materials. There was an enormous amount of preliminary work before the couple ever paid a penny. When they were finished and the contract was signed, Jay told Alex and Beth that the price on the contract was the price of the job, and unless both sides agreed to changes during the work that might alter the cost, they would not be paying any more.

As the contractor in "The Perfect Match," and as someone who averages 100 remodeling jobs a year, Jay Cipriani is probably the best source for what to look for when you hire a professional to spend months in your house and to whom you will be handing over great quantities of money to pay for the work.

The first question you should ask is how long the contractor has been in business. Try to find one who has been in business for at least 10 years because, according to Jay, "95 percent of all contractors go out of business in 3 to 5 years," and you need a longer guarantee than that on the work. The selection process should also include checking references to make sure they are specific and legitimate, not simply lip service paid by someone who could be the contractor's friend or relative. A lot of homeowners will try to get past the bad experiences once the remodeling job is complete, but you need to know if the contractor kept to the job schedule, if it started on time and was finished on time, and, if not, why.

Did the contractor stay within budget? Are there any complaints against the contractor that have been lodged with the local better business bureau or the state consumer affairs department? Where does the contractor do banking? From what sources does the contractor obtain materials? Check with the local building inspector for recommendations or, if the official will not offer any suggestions, find out if there are contractors the inspector recommends not working with. They aren't really supposed to be offering choices, but Jay suggests that if you take them aside and ask them, the building officials usually will be up front with you. If the contractor has nothing to hide, he or she will be completely up front about everything. The contractor who does all of this is the one with whom you'll feel safe and comfortable.

Jay gave Alex and Beth a list of 100 references and urged the couple to call everyone on the list. He even drove them to see a couple of houses that he had recently completed so that they could talk with the owners about the work, and Jay provided the Cerratos with a 12-page manual outlining procedures and even the basics of remodeling.

Homeowners should be looking for contractors who will take care of obtaining all the necessary permits. The contractors are used to working with the local building officials and know all the hoops they have to jump through, as Jay puts it. The homeowners can pay for the permit by going directly to the building department and writing the checks, but the contractor is typically more qualified to fill out all the forms and then provide the sealed drawings that most municipalities require for remodeling work.

Whether or not the contractor applies for the work permit, he or she is still required to make sure that it was done and done correctly. If the building official shows up for an inspection, the contractor cannot plead ignorance. Otherwise, the work will be stopped until the permitting process has been completed to the official's satisfaction. The contract should spell out who is responsible for what, and what should be included in the permit should be detailed in the contract.

One of the biggest choices homeowners have to make concerns materials that are needed for the remodeling job. There are too many choices these days—manufacturer, model number, size, color—and all of that has to be specified in the contract. The contractor generally provides all the materials for the job, and that's a good idea, because he or she will be responsible for making sure that the materials get to the job site on time and that they are exactly what the homeowners wanted. If the item shows up and it is broken, or if it is the wrong one, then it should be the contractor's job to return the item quickly and obtain a replacement to keep the project on schedule. Sometimes the contractor might mark up the price of the item, sometimes not, but the added cost is usually justified by the work the contractor has to do to get the material on-site on time.

The contractor should provide warranty papers to the homeowners on all the materials used in the remodeling project before the agreement is signed and the work begins. The homeowners should know before the product is purchased and installed under what conditions it will be repaired or replaced if something happens to the item over a specified time. That way, if a product has a better warranty than the one the homeowners are requesting, they cannot complain after the fact that such information had not been made available to them to make an informed decision.

Homeowners should be looking for detailed contracts, right down to the size, make, and model of every item or material to be used or installed. Are you getting metal switch-plate covers or plastic switch-plate covers; hollow-core or solid-core interior doors; double-pane, low-E windows or historic wood windows with grilles? Sometimes you may have to do that work for the contractor because they usually have better "hand skills," as Jay puts it, rather than management or typing abilities.

The contract should include the start and completion dates. Some homeowners will include a bonus for a job finished early or on time, or a penalty if it isn't. To obtain the bonus or avoid the penalty, even a reliable contractor might be tempted to cut corners to make the additional money or not lose any, so it's not a good idea. There should be a detailed payment schedule included in the contract. Never give a contractor a huge deposit up front; try to work out an agreement that the contractor will be paid when each phase of the work is completed to your satisfaction.

Always leave a balance at the end of the job to cover punch-list items, which are things that the contractor must come back to fix, such as popped nails in drywall or a door that doesn't close properly. Don't give away all of your money before the job is completed to your satisfaction. Make sure that the contractor and the contractor's subs have the proper amount of insurance to protect you from any injuries or damages that occur on the job, including general liability in case someone backs into your car, and that all laborers are covered by a workers' compensation program in case one of them is injured on the job.

All of these items should be in the contract. If you need help writing a contract, or you want to make sure that the one you are about to sign is the one that offers you the most protection, hire a lawyer. Make sure that the lawyer is willing to assume responsibility for you if a problem requiring litigation arises during or after the job.

One of the major reasons why contractors and homeowners butt heads is over change orders, which are unexpected additional costs for which a homeowner has to pay. Typically, a change order is written up as a work order that specifies additional costs. Jay recommends that before signing the final contract, homeowners should ask the contractor the following questions: "What unforeseen costs could we run into? Can you let us know about it now so we can put money to cover it into our budget?"

Most contractors don't make much money on change work orders because most homeowners already are upset that there is an extra cost. When a contractor discovers that there is a change work order, the contractor typically has to halt work, make changes, and then wait for the delivery of the new materials. Change orders should be written up on a separate piece of paper in detail—including price—and then appended to the original contract. The signatures of both the contractor and the homeowners should be on that change order.

When a dispute arises, it usually is the result of one side or the other failing to communicate. The homeowners have some remedies, including first trying to negotiate with the contractor. If that doesn't work, the next step could be the better business bureau's arbitration board or some third party; then hiring a lawyer to deal directly with the contractor to get the dispute resolved or filing a complaint or a lawsuit if it is not. If the project ends and a problem remains, hang on to your money and don't make any further payments until the matter is resolved or, as Jay advises, "until there is a win-win situation for both parties." Try to work it out at the start. Don't let a bad situation get worse by not communicating with one another.

Beth acknowledges that the work took longer than promised—11 weeks instead of 6 to 8—but there were substantial weather delays that forced workers to be on the job on Saturdays because municipal law prohibits Sunday work. Still, the additional 3 weeks was more than compensated for by the quality of the work and the expertise of Jay's crew and the subs who work for him regularly.

In *What No One Ever Tells You About Renovating Your Home*, I suggested that finding a contractor by word of mouth from friends, neighbors, and family worked most of the time, and I stand by that. I also recommended that you get at least three estimates before you choose a contractor, and I stand by that, too, even though I know that despite 25 years of stressing the importance of returning phone calls promptly, most contractors don't.

Unless the basement is filling up with water, however, take your time finding and hiring a contractor, plumber, electrician, or whomever you need for your job. Only the careful homeowners will find the perfect match.

Flush with Success

> **❝I think all bathrooms should be self-cleaning.❞**
>
> **—Bari Shor, real estate agent and condo owner**

It has become very clear that you just can't have too many bathrooms—even if they are unable to clean themselves. In the past 30 years, household size has fallen to 2.58 from 3.35, but in those same 30 years, the proportion of homes built with fewer than two bathrooms has fallen from 41 percent to just 4 percent.

What is more, if they can figure out how to do it, existing homeowners want the bathrooms that new home buyers are getting, but without the expense of buying new. The result: In 2004, $23.7 billion was spent to build or renovate bathrooms—$7.2 billion alone on renovations.

There are a variety of motivations for change. Bari decided to get rid of her bathtub after she realized that "with life so fast paced these days, I didn't have the time to sit in the tub." Her contractor replaced the bathtub with a walk-in shower with multiple heads—three stationary and one adjustable—and a pie-shaped seat.

Denise and Lane tackled their bathroom after Denise looked up at the living room ceiling

> For many years, the standard bathroom was 5 feet by 8 feet. Today, 10 by 15 or 20 feet is the rule in new houses and in additions to older ones, and this gives the homeowners a chance to create a spa that's separate from the usual facilities, generally as part of a master suite.

> For maximum pressure and minimal loss of heat, supply lines should be three-quarter inches in diameter. The fewer elbow joints used for corners, the lower the resistance in the flow of water to the showerheads.

A soaking tub and shower has a cedar slat floor.

A sink with a view provides plenty of natural light for this high-end bathroom.

A cherry wood vanity with porcelain sink has a granite countertop.

A large mirror and plenty of light to shave is a major feature of this bathroom remodel.

and saw a small stain: "As the leak in the bathtub grew larger, the stain just started getting bigger, so I told Lane that this might be a good time for a bathroom renovation."

Unlike Bari, Denise wanted a new tub because she considered the existing one old and ugly and 4½-feet long—so ugly that she couldn't even remember the last time she had taken a bath. That tub was replaced by the smallest Jacuzzi made, but it was still too large to bring up the narrow stairs of their 11½-foot-wide townhouse. The solution was to lift it up and through the second-floor bathroom window. Once the bathtub was in the room, the contractor had to remove a corner cabinet to fit the tub in place.

Matt spent weekends and weeknights after work for four to five months renovating the only bathroom in his 1892 Queen Anne–style Victorian-era house, finishing it the week before his wedding. His motivation: His fiancée, Judie, had made it clear that she would not move into the house until the bathroom was in perfect working order.

The bathroom, which dated from the early 20th century and had been remodeled a few times in slightly more than 90 years, was not in terrible shape when Matt began his efforts to restore it. In fact, the bathroom had retained many of the features of the late Victorian era,

> If your current tub is big enough but you want to upgrade to a soaking tub or a whirlpool, measure the space anyway, or have your contractor do it. New tubs differ in width from older ones; the new arrival may fit lengthwise between two walls but may create an obstacle in other ways.

> If you're planning to buy a larger tub, the experts suggest trying out as many as you can in the showroom to determine the most comfortable fit. You can do this by lying in the tubs with your clothes on, shoes off.

Left: A two-piece low-flush toilet shares a space with a bidet.

Above: A bidet is becoming a fixture in higher-end bathroom renovations.

More Do-It-Yourself Tips Online!

For a tour of the restored Queen Anne house and interviews with its owners, go to www.remodelingonthemoney.com

A brass vessel sink creates an interesting look in a bathroom.

This rainshower model can be adjusted to provide a gentle spray or a cloudburst.

including a large cast-iron tub—although the tub feet were actually the heads of dolphins instead of the more common claw feet—a stained-glass window, and the original wainscoting, even though that paneling, in Matt's words, had been covered with 800 coats of paints that he had to strip before getting it to the original oak for staining.

If you choose to paint your bathroom, look for a paint designed to fight mold and mildew caused by high moisture levels. If you wallpaper, use vinyl rather than paper for the same reason.

Before beginning a bathroom renovation, have the plumbing checked out completely, even if it means breaking into the walls to check the supply lines and the drain lines. Delays and even higher costs can result if additional plumbing problems occur during construction.

Surprisingly, for an older house, the plumbing was in good shape. Before he began his efforts to restore the bathroom, Matt made certain that "all the water supply lines were copper and not cast iron because cast iron will rust and fall apart, and you don't want to be in the middle of a renovation with plumbing collapsing all about you."

Denise and Lane's bathroom, now 6-feet long and 3-feet wide, cost $6,000 and included glass doors along the tub for the shower; a low-flow, low-profile toilet from France called a *porche*; a 10-inch green porcelain sink with a gray granite top; high-hat lighting; Belgian Arte wallpaper; and space-saving cabinets. That was the low bid. The high bid was $25,000 for the same work. *Remodeling* magazine reports that for a midrange bathroom (redoing a 5-foot-by-7-foot room but not expanding it), the national average cost was $10,499 in 2005.

■ BATHTUBS

The claw-foot, er, dolphin head–foot tub that was the centerpiece of Matt's bathroom renovation/restoration was made of durable cast iron. Reproductions of these tubs often start at $1,500, so if you have one in good

■ Fast Facts on Buying a Bathtub

You must know the dimensions of the space you have to accommodate a new tub, unless you're planning a major reconstruction of your bathroom and can design the space to fit whatever catches your eye.

If you buy a bigger tub, you must know if your house will be able to support it. If not, something will have to be done to reinforce the floor so your second-floor master bath doesn't end up in the first-floor foyer.

Ask your contractor to determine which way the floor joists run, and check with an engineer about adding extra structural support for the tub as needed. To be factored in are the weight of the tub, the people using it, and the water, tile, plumbing, and fixtures. Leave this job to the professionals.

If you're adding a tub, make sure that you're getting enough water supply to the bathroom and that the drainage system can handle all that extra wetness. (This is another job for the pros). Be sure to add insulation around the supply and drain lines to reduce the noise of flowing water.

If you have a 40-gallon water heater and buy a tub that holds 60 gallons, you're likely to run short. And if the supply lines to the tub travel through uninsulated spaces, a lot of heat will be lost. Raising the temperature of the heater is a waste of money so you might consider a supplemental demand or tankless heater (electric or gas) for just the tub, or maybe the entire bathroom.

Tubs come in different materials, and some are more durable than others. For everyday use, you'll likely be looking at models in acrylic, porcelain, fiberglass, and cast iron. Fiberglass is cheap, but not very durable. Cast iron is pricey, but can last a century. Porcelain and acrylic fall in between, in both price and durability.

Color and style are important when you're redoing a bathroom, but the tub is the focal point—it will stand out no matter what, so it doesn't have to match exactly. If you can't find what you want at the home center or plumbing-supply stores, check online for looks that enhance your style, rather than merely coordinate with it.

Cost depends on size, material, and shape, as well as the extras you want—a standard tub versus a soaking tub with jets, for example. Bathtubs can run from $200 to several thousand; a quality standard tub minus the fixtures runs about $700 to $1,000.

 Watch as an old bathtub is turned into a new one at www.remodelingonthemoney.com

A jet Jacuzzi fits into a wood cabinet.

An air jet tub has a headrest for complete soaking comfort.

shape, hold on to it. You may have to replace the faucets (there are less pricey reproductions available) and the drain line, and may wish to add a shower to make the tub completely useful. Shower conversion kits range in price from $100 to about $500, depending on the style and material, and include a shower curtain attachment that mounts to the bathroom wall.

Koehler's multispray shower can be programmed at various spray rates (Photo courtesy of Kohler).

If the old tub isn't in such good shape, and having to remove it will increase the cost of the renovation project without an adequate payback, you should consider having the tub refinished, if that is possible. There are a number of do-it-yourself refinishing products available in home centers and hardware stores—most involve a two-part epoxy system, cost between $35 and $60, and are designed for refinishing porcelain sinks as well as tubs—but if you are spending $15,000 on a bathroom renovation, you want your refinishing job to come with at least a five-year warranty.

Professional refinishers use different methods. One involves sandblasting the outside, then

> After the waterlines have been reconnected, the plumber should run the outside hose valve and flush toilets to expel dirt and air from those lines. If this is not done, any remaining debris can clog the faucets in your sink and tub and the showerheads.

using a two-part etching primer after repairing nicks and scratches with a waterproof fiberglass filler. Prices for refinishing tubs start at $500 with an additional $50 for changing the color of the tub. The old faucet holes can be removed if you want the fixtures changed. The standard warranty is 5 years; most refinishing jobs typically last 15 or more, depending on how well you care for the tub.

Most do-it-yourself porcelain restoration kits provide enough epoxy for one tub or two sinks. Surface preparation, including sanding the surface for better adhesion, is critical to the success of the process, and treatment involves at least two coats of epoxy—the first thin, the second thicker.

A multispray is controlled by two levers.

The focus on bathtubs is part of a trend over the past five years to create home spas. The thinking behind the home spa, despite Bari's decision to replace her tub with a shower, is that women want a place to relax in privacy, and they don't have the time to spend each day at the spa.

A must-have in many sanctuaries is a soaking tub separate from the bathtub or shower that others use, but most buyers prefer simple shapes, and that means a whirlpool tub, which remains the number-one choice. A close second, however, is the air jet, in which air is propelled through

Three showerheads in this unit with separate controls. Requirements can be programmed in for each user (Photo courtesy of Koehler).

A multispray head in the ceiling of a shower.

dozens of small holes for an all-over bubbling action. Unlike a whirlpool, aromatherapy oils and salts can be added and emitted from the jets into the water.

As Bari's experience suggests, whether the bathroom has a tub is a matter of taste. Many architects and designers are reporting a shift away from tubs to the high-tech, multiple-head, walk-in shower that Bari chose. Bari is a veteran real estate agent, however, and even she acknowledges that her decision to chuck the tub for the high-tech shower isn't a decision to be made lightly. She had decided that she was not planning to move any time soon so "the decision was made for me, and not how it might affect resale of the unit when the time comes."

Kohler's controller can be programmed for every user's needs (Photo courtesy of Kohler).

Before you refinish an old tub, make sure it is worth refinishing or can be spruced up for that matter. If the original tub cost $200, there is no reason to spend $500 or more restoring it. Look for good porcelain. You can always clean the outside, but resurfacing is a temporary measure, considering the length of most warranties. When you resurface, you aren't putting on a coat of porcelain but epoxy resin, which is car paint.

■ UPGRADING THE SHOWER

Tubs are in no danger of going away, so if you have the room in your remodeled bathroom, don't leave the bathtub out. However, many designers are also including steam immersion showers and shower towers, and "rain baths" with elegant fixtures. Frosted-glass enclosures with minimal hardware and interior lighting make them look like glass boxes.

Kohler is known for its integrated one-piece, custom shower units known as "towers," but in April 2006, it entered the bathroom-as-spa sweepstakes with a bit of technology

Designer sink with a single faucet by Kohler fits on a shelf (Photo courtesy of Kohler).

called the DTV—a touch screen ($2,000) that allows multiple users to program their shower preferences, such as temperature, pressure, and up-and-down massage.

At the same time, Moen introduced an ExactTemp Thermostatic Valve that allows you to dial a precise water temperature on demand. The valve itself costs about $250, but that's just part of a package. For example, the ShowHouse by Moen Waterhill ExactTemp with Five Function Transfer Valve Vertical Spa Set in nickel ($2,700).

ProSun International, manufacturer of tanning equipment, has incorporated ultraviolet lamps and filters in its Sunshower, which promises to tan your skin while you wash ($10,000).

The inexpensive way of getting more—or better performance—out of your shower is by changing the showerhead to one of the many "rainshower" heads on the market. Once confined

> Some fixture manufacturers are now combining the whirlpool and air jet functions in their tubs, which start at $5,000. Separately, starting prices are $2,000.

> Ceramic wall tile can be repainted with proper preparation and the right kind of paint. Cleaning and surface preparation are the key, after which you should apply a high-adhesion primer and a high-quality finish paint. Acrylic latex is often acceptable, but high-moisture areas may require an epoxy paint. Ask the people in the paint department of your local home center what's best for you.

Jacuzzi offers a frame that allows a video screen to be adjusted as you adjust to your bath (Photo courtesy of Jacuzzi).

A hideway place in the bathroom for dirty clothes.

To have a plastic or fiberglass one-piece shower stall installed will range in cost from $800 to $1,800, depending on whether demolition and/or plumbing changes are required. A walk-in, glass-enclosed shower stall with a ceramic tile interior starts at $2,000, including labor.

If the drain line is not pitched properly—one inch for every four feet—stagnant water can collect and smell. The presence of hydrogen sulfide often lends a rotten-egg smell to the water. Hydrogen sulfide is typically found in water heaters because the heat dissolves the gases that exist naturally in groundwater so the smell would appear when you turned on the hot water. You may have to flush the heater regularly to clean out the sediment that collects.

to the stalls of high-end hotel rooms, just about every manufacturer has a version on the market.

■ LIGHTING YOUR BATHROOM

While we are on the subject of fans, it is time to figure out what the bathroom needs in the way of illumination. Too much light and you ruin your makeup. Too little and you miss a few spots shaving.

■ CHOOSING A HOT WATER HEATER

Additional demand requires more, especially hot, water, and you'll need to figure out first whether the existing water heater is capable of supplying more. Most three-bedroom houses have 40-gallon storage water heaters. The question is, will that be big enough to fill a 100-gallon bathtub after the dishes are done and in the dead of winter?

For the past few years, more homeowners remodeling bathrooms have turned to gas or electric tankless, or "on-demand," water heaters. Although tankless water heaters have been in use in Europe and Asia for years, they have only recently arrived here.

Tankless units heat and deliver water on demand. Cold water is circulated through a series of burners or electric coils that heat the water as it passes through. There is no storage tank. Tankless units cost more than storage heaters, but because you are not heating a big tank of water 24 hours a day, they cost less to operate.

A mosaic vessel sink fits easily into a granite countertop.

■ Fast Facts on Rainshowers

"Rainshower" means just that: a gentle flow that falls softly on the user below. The water pressure a rainshower head produces is neither strong enough nor concentrated enough to wash the soap off your hair and body quickly. If you want to spend less time in the shower, you'll have to buy something other than the standard, gravity-fed rainshower head.

If a thundershower is more to your liking, you'll need an adjustable showerhead with several settings—the greater the number, the higher the price—that are more forceful because the spray is concentrated through fewer holes.

Taking the hint, some manufacturers are offering rainshower heads that are a bit more powerful. Moen's "immersion rainshower-style showerhead" are pressurized to send a powerful flow through individual spray channels. Grohe's Tempesta hand rainshower has a very wide spray face for maximum water coverage. Dornbracht's BigRain system can be installed in the ceiling to simulate a storm instead of just a sprinkle. Still other manufacturers offer multiple rainshower-head systems.

Size does matter. Is your shower stall or bathtub big enough to accommodate a rainshower head? If the space is too small, the showerhead might extend too far from the wall and miss you completely while spilling water outside, or the rainshower might so dominate the space that you have no choice

but to wash your hair every time you step underneath it. A smaller-diameter showerhead might be the answer; standard models range from 6 inches to 12 inches. Handheld models also are available.

Weight also matters because rainshower heads are heavier, and they need extra support to keep even the slightest water pressure from pushing them down. Follow installation instructions to the letter, and use the recommended hardware.

Because rainshower heads have more holes, they are more likely to become clogged by impurities in the water, which will reduce water flow even further. For cleaning, most sources recommend soaking the showerhead overnight in vinegar and water and then reinstalling.

Some newer models come with disposable filter cartridges that reduce clogging, but you'll need to replace those filters regularly for the showerhead to work properly.

Rainshower heads look a lot like camp showers, with a retro feel that can fit in with both traditional and contemporary bathroom decor. They come in a variety of finishes, too: chrome, of course, but also brass, brushed nickel, and a "weathered copper" offered by Benson.

As with everything, you pay for style. You can buy a rainshower head for as little as $30 and as much as $500 for high-end finishes and add-ons.

With all that steam being generated, don't forget the exhaust fan. Moisture can be a problem in the bathroom. It can cause paint to peel, doors to warp, and the accumulation of mold spores. A simple exhaust fan can greatly reduce or eliminate the many problems created by excess moisture. Installing a fan/light combination as a replacement for an existing light fixture is an easy project. The wiring is already in place. Other options include a humidity sensor, timer (20 minutes should be enough time to remove shower-created moisture), and reduced sound (measured in sones—fewer sones, less sound). Price range: $150 to $300.

Heating water accounts for 20 percent or more of a typical household's annual energy expenditures, according to the U.S. Department of Energy. The yearly operating costs for conventional storage-tank water heaters average $200 for gas units, $450 for electric ones.

Storage-tank water heaters raise the water temperature to the setting on the tank, usually between 120 and 140 degrees, and maintain it there. Even if no hot water is drawn from the tank (and cold water enters the tank), the heater will operate periodically to maintain the temperature. This is the result of what are called standby losses—the heat conducted and radiated from the walls of the tank and, in gas-fired water heaters, through the flue pipe. Standby losses represent 10 to 20 percent of a household's annual water-heating costs.

By providing hot water immediately where it is used, tankless heaters waste less water: You

■ Fast Facts on Bathroom Lighting

For best results, you want diffused, softer light in the bathroom.

Use lighter colors on walls and accents because they reflect light and let it bounce around the room.

Using the correct fluorescent will create a better reflection off surfaces and help you see yourself in true light.

Avoid "Hollywood" lights above a mirror because they cast horrible shadows. Instead, light both sides of the mirror evenly for a balanced spread of light and for improved visibility while applying makeup.

If using vanity strips with globe lights, choose frosted instead of clear to help minimize shadows.

For fans of reading in the bathtub, an enclosed luminaire at least six feet above the waterline offers good reading light and ensures safety.

do not need to let the water run as you wait for warmer water to reach a remote faucet. Equipment life may be longer than with tank-type heaters because tankless models are less subject to corrosion. The expected life of tankless water heaters is 20 years, compared with 10 to 15 years for tank-type heaters. Tankless heaters range in price from $200 for a small under-sink unit to $1,000 for a gas-fired unit that delivers 5 gallons per minute. Those numbers do not include installation, which can add $150 to $300 to the price.

A few plumbers with experience in older tankless models complain that the heating coils are prone to rusting, but improvements have been made in the newest generation to prevent the problem. A lot of plumbers, like many other contractors (and most people), tend to be set in their ways. It is much easier to pick up a tank water heater at the plumbing-supply house, take out the old one, and put in the new than it is to devote time to learning about alternatives.

> Speaking of mirrors, the full-length variety is already an important part of the spa culture. And so, for some, are flat-screen televisions. Multitaskers being introduced include Myson's line of Aquavision mirrored TV/towel warmers. Turn off the 17-by-12-inch TV and it becomes a mirror ($6,000 to $6,500).

> Looking for entertainment in the bath? Jacuzzi's Lift-It is an aluminum-frame elevation system that, at the push of a button, lets you raise, lower, or store a plasma TV screen from the tub ($1,709 for the Horizon model, which accommodates a 27-inch screen; $2,729 for the Crest model, which handles a 42-inch screen).

Rinnai's on-demand tankless water heater (Photo courtesy of Rinnai).

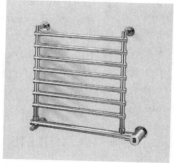

A towel warmer fits easily on a bathroom wall.

A dual-flush toilet is designed to save water.

Remember that it is what you want that is important, not what the contractor or the subcontractor wants, because you are the person paying and the one who will be using the space.

If you cannot find a plumber willing or able to install a tankless heater in your house, contact the manufacturer for names of installers in your area.

In high-moisture areas such as bathrooms, ground fault circuit interrupter (GFCI) receptacles should be installed. GFCIs constantly monitor electricity flowing in a circuit. If the electricity flowing into the circuit differs by even a slight amount from that returning, the GFCI will quickly shut off the current flowing through that circuit. The advantage of using GFCIs is that they can detect even small variations in the amount of leakage current, even amounts too small to activate a fuse or circuit breaker. Older receptacles should be replaced by GFCIs. They cost about $80 to $150 installed.

Building new walls in the bathroom? Make sure that the contractor uses material that holds up better to those high levels of moisture than standard drywall. Two suggestions: greenboard and tile backer board, which both stand up to dampness.

Typically, the more hot water a unit produces, the higher the cost. Electric tankless heaters typically cost more to operate than gas units. Some drawbacks to demand water heating include the following:

Unless your demand system has a feature called modulating temperature control, it may not heat water to a constant temperature at different flow rates. That means that water temperatures can fluctuate uncomfortably, particularly if the pressure varies wildly in your water system.

Electric units will draw more instantaneous power than tank-type water heaters. If electric rates include a demand charge, operation may be expensive. Electric units also require a relatively high power draw because water must be heated quickly to the desired temperature. Make sure your wiring is up to the demand.

■ BATHROOM SINKS

Replacing the bathroom sink can mean many decisions. Can you, for instance, add (or enhance) storage at the same time by installing a new sink/vanity combination? Or maybe you don't have enough room for a vanity and must select a pedestal sink, or one that hangs from the wall or tucks into a corner.

■ TOILETS

There is a trend in bathroom design that compartmentalizes the toilet, separating it from the sink, shower, and tub by a wall or screen. It is a good idea from a modesty standpoint,

■ Fast Facts on Sinks

You need to be aware of exactly how much space you're dealing with, though simply taking measurements and finding something that fits isn't the whole story either. The sink you select should be in proportion to all the other fixtures in the bathroom to allow ease of movement. Plus, the sink (and accompanying vanity, if you can accommodate one) should be of a style compatible with the existing fixtures, unless you're planning to change them, too.

Bathroom sinks get a lot of use, so considering the user is important. You might hesitate to put a fancy vessel sink made of glass, copper, or bronze (best reserved for guests) in a place where the resident handyman washes off after painting the walls. Likewise, you might want a durable, easy-to-clean sink made of cast iron or vitreous china in the bathroom your kids use.

Whatever the composition of your sink, you need to know what to use to clean it. Some sink finishes are so delicate that even the prospect of Comet cleanser and a scrub brush will scar them for life. If the sales staff where you shop can't tell you, go to the manufacturer's website. If you've already bought a sink, look at the manufacturer's warranty, which will be invalidated if you do the wrong thing and scuff it up.

For wall-mount and pedestal sinks, prices start at about $100 and go to $1,200 because of the variety of styles and materials available. A midrange drop-in sink for a vanity will cost $150 to $400.

If you're planning to spend a long time in your current house, consider buying a sink that would work for you if you were in a wheelchair.

Pedestal and wall-mounted sinks offer little nonbasin surface area and no storage.

Sometimes, a table or desk can be retrofitted to hold a small sink and still offer enough room for a soapdish and a toothbrush holder.

Standard (not custom-built) vanities range in width from 18 to 48 inches; they come in 6-inch increments (24, 30, 36, 42, and 48 inches wide) and a variety of woods and finishes. Cabinets are either traditional face frame with standard hinges or frameless European cabinets with adjustable hinges.

A vanity requires you to add a countertop and hardware to your list of purchases. Laminate countertops are the least expensive choice but they can scratch. Stone is durable but pricey.

You'll need to coordinate your faucet choices with the style of the rest of the bathroom. If you have a room with a bit of age to it, the task might not be that easy. If your bathroom has remained intact from the 1920s, you're in luck—many manufacturers are making reproduction faucets in that style. If your bathroom is of midcentury vintage, say 1950 to 1970, you may have some trouble finding period styles.

What you end up with will be determined not only by availability and price, but by whether the sink you've bought comes with predrilled holes. If it does, standard distances are 4 inches, 8 inches, and single hole. Widespread faucets are for sinks with centers between 8 inches and 16 inches.

Pop-up drains are designed for easy cleaning, but beware: If you don't know what you're doing, the screw on the pop-up mechanism can become too tight to allow proper drainage. Drains need to be cleaned regularly; otherwise, soap and hair will collect and water will drain more slowly.

especially if the house can accommodate a single bathroom for more than one user. It does nothing, however, to address the nearly two-decade-old debate over the shortcomings of low-flow toilets now required by law in residential uses.

■ Fast Facts on Toilets

How well does it flush? Flushability is determined by how successfully the design works within federal standards mandating a reduction in the number of gallons of water needed. The law reduced the amount to 1.6 gallons from 3 or 7 gallons, but the first versions of the low-flow toilets did not do the job as designed. Needing to flush a low-flow more than once defeats the purpose of the law.

A dual-flush toilet offers a 1-gallon-or-less flush for liquid waste, 1.6 gallons for solid waste. Most newer models replace the rubber flapper, which is prone to degrading, with a silicon gasket and calibrated plunger. Their bowls and trapways have been redesigned to work better.

There's still debate over whether the "wash-down" flush, which relies on gravity and a wide trapway, or the "siphonic," which uses suction and a narrow passage, works best, but all you want to know is whether one flush will do it. Some single-flush, low-flow toilets use pressurized air to force water into the bowl. Pressure-assisted toilets are noisier than gravity-flush models, and some must be plugged into an electrical outlet.

Low-flow toilets with larger trapways work better. (Trapways can be found on both sides of the toilet; they look like tubes.)

Do you want a one-piece toilet or a two-piece model? In two-piece toilets, bowl and tank are separate entities; one-piece models combine them. A one-piece toilet is easier to clean because there's no crevice between the tank and the bowl. Some toilets come with sanitary bars that prevent liquid from collecting under the tank at the back of the bowl.

Size and shape do matter. Toilets are available in several different dimensions, depending on the amount of clearance to the wall behind the toilet needed to connect the waterline. Twelve inches is the most common. Round toilets are smaller and save space. Elongated, or oval, toilets provide a larger seating area, but they're 2 inches longer, so be sure your space can accommodate an oval. Older buyers may prefer a bowl that is between 14 and 17 inches above the floor, for more comfortable use.

When it comes to price, don't skimp. There are a lot of cheap toilets available, and you get what you pay for. Some toilets will last 30 years or more, but the experts put the average at 10 to 15 years. The fixture itself will last much longer than its parts, which need regular replacement. Depending on how it flushes—vacuum, pressure assist, gravity, and single or dual flush—a typical home toilet can run $150 to $400.

■ BATHROOM HARDWARE

Some people spruce up their kitchens by changing the hardware on cabinet doors and drawers. In bathrooms, the same can be accomplished with new faucets.

What about the self-cleaning bathroom? Of course, only those kiosks on the streets of Paris can do that. On the other hand, one expert has suggested that if

---

■ Fast Facts on Faucets

You should determine which style will work best for your family, from young children to elderly parents. Levers instead of twist knobs might be advisable for the latter. Two-handle, center-set faucets (one handle for hot water, one for cold) typically are used for bathroom sinks. Single-handle faucets (handle position determines water temperature) once were mostly found in kitchens, but these days they're used in bathrooms, too.

Question: "If I want to, can I replace my two-handle faucet with a single-handle unit?" Answer: Sink openings and faucet dimensions are standardized now so you usually can. But there are exceptions (old-house owners, take note), so it's a good idea to check sizes first. Many single- and two-handle faucets in bathroom sinks are on 4-inch centers (the distance between the centers of the hot and cold inlets or mounting bolts). Two-handle faucets with spreads of 8 to 16 inches are available and feature flexible hookups.

You can buy a faucet for $30, or you can buy one for $800, but price dictates quality. Though manufacturers acknowledge that the upper end of the market sets trends in design and finishes, they say the typical American household buys somewhere in the $90 to $250 range, with chrome the most popular finish.

You'll definitely pay more for high style. Moen has introduced a pewter finish and Price Pfister has unveiled distressed "rustic bronze" and "rustic pewter" finishes designed to appear weathered with age. Another new trend is toward the "architecturally inspired" faucet, something that might have been in a Roman bath or a 19th-century farmyard.

Some finishes aren't easy to maintain. If you have neither the time nor the inclination to preserve a sheen or patina, consider a dull finish over one you have to spend time polishing.

Gooseneck faucets, common in kitchens with deep sinks for pot scrubbing, are a good idea for the bathroom, too, especially if you have a coffeemaker in your master suite.

Keep a copy of the installation instructions and parts list as well as the warranty information for your new faucet. The more it cost, the more likely that a $3 to $15 part will fix a future problem.

Waterless urinals are a great idea for public facilities, but they are not a common feature of residential bathrooms yet because, despite efforts by many manufacturers to encourage their use in the home, bathroom style trends tend to lean more toward the bidet. The waterless urinals install to the regular waste lines, but eliminate the flush water-supply lines. Flush valves also are eliminated. The bowl surfaces repel waste liquid.

you spent just three and one-half minutes each day wiping down the bathroom, you'd never have to schedule a major cleaning again.

"I don't even have three and a half minutes a day," Bari says. "If I did, I'd have kept the bathtub."

Everything *and* the Kitchen Sink

2

The lion's share of bells and whistles are finding their way to the modern kitchen, and while the experts suggest that the typical consumer doesn't replace a big-ticket item such as a refrigerator until it breaks, the appliance manufacturers spend considerable effort coming up with new products designed to convince the same consumer that what he or she owns isn't good enough, and to abandon a satisfactory and reasonably priced model with something new, exciting, and, of course, more expensive.

A dishwasher should provide racks that accommodate plenty of dishes.

There is no overwhelming evidence that the typical homeowner will spend anywhere from $15,000 to $80,000 remodeling a kitchen simply to accommodate a refrigerator with a built-in television set or Internet access. The decision to spend that kind of money usually results from a change in lifestyle. For Allison and Scott, the new kitchen was part of a two-story addition to better accommodate a family of five.

19

If cared for properly, a dishwasher will last as many as 12 years; a garbage disposal, about 13; an oven, close to 20.

"We wanted the kitchen to open up into the family room to maximize the space by getting rid of the walls," Scott said, "but we didn't want to forgo a dining room. So we created a dining room space to the right of the kitchen, used the kitchen island as a dividing line between the kitchen and the family room, and used the space from the old and small kitchen for a computer room and a half bath. In that way, the kids can play under supervision or we can help them with their homework if we have things to do in the kitchen."

A bottom freezer in GE's Profile refrigerator (Photo courtesy of GE).

Cabinets should provide plenty of storage, and everything stored should be easily accessible.

Beth and Alex had the same needs as Scott and Allison—their house was about half the size of what they found they needed when sons Cole and Ben arrived—but they came to a different decision on what to do.

"We had more need of a living room than a dining room, so we used the dining room space to create a large kitchen area that has a counter with stools between support columns that replaced the load-bearing wall that divided the old kitchen and the wall," Beth said. "The family room surrounds the kitchen on three sides and overlooks the deck, accessible through French doors. That way I can watch the boys while I'm cooking, even if they are playing out on the deck."

Kitchen designers say that cooks want to be placed in the middle of family activities so they can keep tabs on what everyone is doing. Kitchens these days are almost always open to the family room and often have wide views of the outside. They also are getting larger because cooking has become a social activity with more than one preparation area and more than one kitchen. People who do a lot of entertaining want a party kitchen with large open areas that allow guests enough room to mingle.

> If you want a larger kitchen but don't have the space, one option is to turn a living room into a formal dining room and incorporate the space from the old dining room into the kitchen.

While the need for new and bigger space motivates kitchen renovation, the typical consumer spends huge amounts of time trying to decide what to put into that added square footage. Dennis, a remodeling contractor, averages 150 to 170 remodeling jobs a year with 80 percent

A convection oven bakes evenly and quickly as the fan in the rear spreads the heat.

A warming drawer is considered a "lower oven."

involving kitchens and baths in one way or another. Knowing full well the number of choices that such an undertaking involves, Dennis took his cue from the new-home builders and came up with a remodeling design center, which features one full-size working kitchen and two smaller ones, a butler's pantry, and an almost-complete working master bath and spa.

> Big-ticket kitchen appliance manufacturers continue to report a 20 to 25 percent increase in sales of their products each year.

Don't forget that new appliances and an expanded modern kitchen have greater power needs than the older models, so have a licensed electrician determine your needs. Some appliances require dedicated circuits to operate efficiently and properly. A lot of older houses require upgraded electrical service, and if the electrician determines that the proposed changes will require a 200-amp service instead of the present 100 amp, expect to add up to $3,000 to the cost of the renovation for the work. Every dedicated circuit will cost from $250 for a 120 volt to $500 for a 240-volt one.

Go shopping for the latest in tankless "on demand" water heaters at www.remodelingonthemoney.com

Kitchens also require more and better lighting, and that adds to the power needs. It is difficult to determine how many fixtures the kitchen will need. The amount of natural light plays a huge factor in lighting design, but you will need adequate lighting over food preparation areas, under cabinets, and in darker places. Installing a standard light fixture can cost about $150 each; receptacles can run from $100 to $250 each, installed.

Innovation in kitchen appliances has made kitchen design easier. Instead of having to work around a traditional stove, the consumer can install a cooktop in the kitchen island and ovens in the wall. Dishwasher drawers allow you to divide the capacity of a single dishwasher in two places. Microwaves have become increasingly smaller and can be installed under the counter rather than on top.

Under-the-counter coolers for drinks and wine (Photo courtesy of GE).

An under-the-counter wine and beverage cooler.

■ REFRIGERATORS

You have two options when you remodel a kitchen. One is to try to fit the appliances you own into the new space. The other, of course, is to buy new.

Kitchens are not just kitchens but living spaces, so it's all about integrating appliances so they look like they belong in places they don't belong.

Because newer models tend to be more energy efficient than older ones—even the ones that seem to work perfectly—refrigerators are usually the number one replacement item in a kitchen remodel in all but the lowest price range.

■ Fast Facts on Refrigerators

Determine how much refrigerator space will meet your needs. Consider the shapes and sizes of items you typically store and how your chilling/ freezing requirements stack up. Look not just at overall capacity, but also at how various bin and shelf options can help you store food efficiently.

When selecting a refrigerator, size does matter. It should be neither too large nor too small. You want one spacious enough for special occasions, of course, but modest enough that you're not running an empty, energy-wasting box the rest of the time. Consider how well the capacity of your current refrigerator suits you, then scale up or down accordingly.

The typical refrigerator provides between 18 and 26 cubic feet of storage space. Models with top and bottom freezers typically have a capacity range of 10 to 22 cubic feet. For a family of four, 19 to 22 cubic feet is ideal. A very large side-by-side model could have a capacity as large as 26 cubic feet.

Freezer capacity can vary quite substantially from model to model. Think about what you store in there and plan accordingly. Prepackaged products (the boxes alone often eat up a lot of freezer space)? Bulk items? Bags of ice? Remember, too, that an icemaker will need space of its own.

Capacity is not the only issue here. Before you shop, be sure to measure carefully the space you have for a new fridge. As houses have gotten bigger, appliances have gotten taller, wider, and deeper. Finding what you want in the size you want is sometimes a challenge, especially if you own an older house. Refrigerators need room to "breathe," so don't squeeze one into a tight spot. Make sure doors and drawers can open without obstruction.

Be sure to ask about energy efficiency. A refrigerator operates nonstop, and in a typical household accounts for 12 to 20 percent of total power used in one year. For this reason, an aging refrigerator is probably costing you money. Many models produced before 1999 don't even meet current U.S. Department of Energy power-usage guidelines. The latest refrigerators use 30 percent less electricity than models built 10 years ago because of better insulation and more efficient compressors and motors.

Once you calculate what fits your needs and what fits your space, you'll have to choose from side-by-side, top-mount, bottom-mount, or compact/under-counter models.

Residential-model side-by-sides range from $800 to $2,500; top freezers, $500 to $2,000. Bottom freezers run from $800 to $2,100; compacts, $150 to $400.

Refrigerator shelves should be sturdy, flexible, and easy to clean. Glass is generally better. Adjustable shelves are a plus; some models have half-shelves that can be matched up for a wide, flat surface or adjusted separately for odd-height items. Look, too, for easy-to-reach temperature and humidity controls.

■ OVENS

■ Fast Facts on Wall Ovens

Wall height determines whether you can include a single or a double oven. Ovens come in widths of 24, 27, and 30 inches. The interior configuration of the oven is important because more rack positions available means more food can be cooked at one time. You want an oven that provides even baking and hides the baking element so that it won't get caked with the splatter of spills.

Manufacturers say convection ovens now account for 30 percent of the market. These electric ovens use a fan in the rear to circulate hot air around the food. There are at least two baking elements that provide the heat; some models have a third element surrounding the fan. The even distribution of consistent heat means that food takes less time to cook. Many convection ovens have conventional bake and broil settings as well as convection options.

Speed ovens combine conventional, microwave, and convection to drastically cut cooking times. The microwave function is ideal for defrosting, reheating, and cooking a variety of food items or for just popping corn. The oven, with its convection mode and browning element, offers roasting and baking functions. The advantage is that you can cook either by microwave or convection or combine the two methods.

Self-cleaning ovens heat up to intensely high temperatures, turning spills in the oven into a fine powder that can be wiped away. The oven securely latches during the cleaning, which can take hours.

A griddle can be accommodated on the middle burner of this gas stove.

GE Monogram five burner stove has a high-heat central burner for accommodating large pans (Photo courtesy of GE).

Prices range from $500 to $2,000 for single and double ovens.

■ COOKTOPS

Cooktops have made kitchen design more flexible, but the wealth of products available has made choosing the right one a difficult task for consumers.

■ WARMING DRAWERS

Never willing to rest on their laurels, appliance manufacturers have come up with a couple of cooking ideas. The first is the warming drawer, which is designed for family members who come in at various times after meals have been cooked.

Three major manufacturers—Sharp, Miele, and Gagganeau—have come up with steam ovens that combine steam with electric heating to produce roasting, grilling, and baking with steam. The result is crisp and moist food. Price: $1,500 to $5,000.

Several manufacturers are offering induction cooktops. Induction uses a magnetic field that's similar to what goes on with a microwave oven. A magnetic pan is used and, underneath it, a magnetic field is created that transfers heat to the pan instead of the glass cooktop itself—even distribution of temperature for even cooking and 90 percent efficiency, compared with 60 percent for gas.

What if you can't guarantee when you'll be home and don't want to wait for something to cook? The answer: Whirlpool's Polara refrigerated range. Say you have a pan of frozen lasagna and you are certain that it will not be thawed for dinner. Then you have to warm it through, and you are now looking at eating at 10 PM. The Polara can be programmed to cool, thawing the lasagna slowly and evenly. Then, at a preprogrammed time, the range will switch to baking mode, making sure that the lasagna is ready when you come home.

The oven will stop baking at a preprogrammed time. If you get held up in traffic, it will kick into warming for an hour. If you get home late and decide

Unusual lighting gives the kitchen an unusual look.

■ Fast Facts on Cooktops

There are gas cooktops and electric ones. They offer many of the same features, including flexible surface heat with high-output burners, enamel surfaces for easy cleaning, and self-ventilation systems or downdraft designs.

Electric cooktops use either standard coil burners or smooth-top ceramic glass in which the heating elements are sealed beneath a solid surface. Electric models provide constant, even heat and, unlike many gas cooktops, let you maintain steady and very low heat.

Gas cooktop burners offer more precise temperature control. You also can see the flame, so you can lower or raise it to a host of temperature settings. Burners cool down and heat up quickly and, unlike electric cooktops, hold little heat when they are off, so cooking stops almost immediately.

Ask yourself these questions: How much do I need to cook at one time? What do I need to cook, and how often? A top-of-the-line cooktop at a top-of-the-line price for heating up takeout food could be a waste of money. Whatever you buy, be sure the cooktop fits the shape and space of your kitchen.

Ceramic-glass electric cooktops have smooth surfaces that are easy to clean and radiant elements that heat up and cool down quickly. These models encase the radiant ele-ments beneath a sheet of ceramic glass. The elements have properties that heat quickly to evenly cook foods. The downside: Radiant elements are generally more expensive than conventional coil-burner cooktops.

Cooktops known as "gas on glass" have smooth-top, ceramic-glass surfaces or a sealed gas cooking system. They feature gas burners placed over a smooth ceramic surface. Gas cooktops are also available in stainless steel.

Both are also easier to clean than open burners or coils.

For a gas cooktop, you will need a hookup either to a natural-gas source or a liquid-propane supply tank. In addition, a model with electronic ignition, an automatic system that instantly lights the burners, will require a 120-volt household electric circuit.

Manufacturers recommend ventilation for both gas and electric cooktops. Either a hood or a microwave/hood combination will provide the vented, nonvented, or recirculating exhaust you'll need to remove cooking odors, smoke, grease, and oil from the air in your kitchen.

Standard electric cooktops cost $150 to $1,000, while gas models run $200 to $1,500. Induction cooktops cost roughly $3,000 to $5,000.

to forgo the lasagna, the range will return to refrigeration for up to 24 hours. The compressor for the refrigerator is in the storage drawer in the bottom of the oven. At 30 inches wide, the stove will fit any standard space. The cost for this luxury: $1,899.

Dacor's microwave drawer.

■ CLEANING UP

Once you've cooked the food and have eaten your fill, you have to take care of the remains of the day—garbage and dishes. Garbage disposals are handy, especially for trapping and grinding bits of food rinsed from the dishes, but your municipality might not allow them, and while there are newer models that are designed to be used with septic systems, many experts say that it is not a good idea. Unless you are running a restaurant, a half-horsepower disposal is enough for the average family's needs. Dishwasher drain lines are typically connected to the garbage disposal so bits of food washed from dishes and utensils can go directly into the machine for grinding. The line is connected to a backflow device that prevents waste in the disposal from returning

To keep the blades of a garbage disposal sharp, grind a tray of ice cubes
once a month. Is there a smell? Look
under the rubber flaps for decompos-
ing food. Grind a lemon and some
baking soda when the need arises.

Washing dishes by hand wastes 5,000
gallons of water a year and takes five
times as long as a dishwasher.

to the dishwasher. A piece of advice: Periodically clean the filter at the bottom of the dishwasher. Large bits of waste can become trapped
at the drain line connection to the disposal, creating a leak. Prices range from about $80 to $500
uninstalled.

Now that the dishes have been scraped
and rinsed, they need to be washed or, better
yet, sterilized, which is the chief attribute of the
mechanical dishwasher. Some dishwashers also
have a feature that sanitizes the dishes by raising the temperature of the water to 150 degrees
Fahrenheit during the final rinse, after the dishes
are completely clean.

A dishwasher consists of an enclosed tub where washing and drying take
place, racks to hold the dishes, a pump to circulate water, a water valve, a heater,
wash arms, and dispensers. The dishwasher first fills with about one and a half
gallons of water. Then a pump circulates this water through wash arms that
rotate below and above the racks that hold the dishes. The water spray from
the wash arms removes food soil from
the dishes. As food soil is removed, it
goes through a food disposer, where it
is chopped into small particles. Water
containing the food particles goes into
a fine mesh filter, where the particles
are trapped. This filter is continually
cleaned by spray holes in one of the
wash arms.

After several minutes of washing, the wash pump stops and a drain

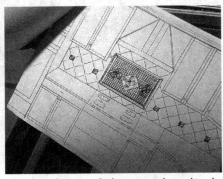

A kitchen design including a wood vent hood.

pump takes over. It draws the food soil out of the filter and pumps it down the
drain along with the water from the tub. Some dishwashers have advanced
sensors to determine how dirty the dishes are by analyzing the water that is
being circulated. The sensor will determine how many fill and drain cycles the
dishwasher will execute.

A heating element heats the water to the proper temperature. Detergent,
which has been put into the detergent dispenser, is discharged into the water at

the proper point in the cycle. The combination of the heated water, detergent, and spray action cleans the dishes. To keep the dishes free of spots, a special rinse aid is dispensed into the final rinse water. At the end of the wash and rinse cycles, the dishes are dried by heating the air in the dishwasher. A dishwasher can fill and drain water from two to six times, depending on the cycle chosen or how dirty the dishes are. Water use varies from 3 to 10 gallons.

A flexible faucet in a kitchen sink.

New dishwashers use about half the electricity of 25-year-old models, according to the U.S. Department of Energy's ENERGY STAR program. They can save time and use about half as much water as hand-washing. Older dishwashers use 8 to 14 gallons of water compared with 3 to 10 gallons for newer models. The efficiency gain for new dishwashers is largely due to improved spray arms and filtering systems that provide better movement and wash action, resulting in decreased hot water use.

While full-size dishwashers are standard in kitchens these days, dishwashers in drawers offer designers more flexibility.

■ Fast Facts on Dishwasher Drawers

Choice is limited to two major manufacturers, Fisher & Paykel and KitchenAid, a division of Whirlpool Corp. Still, you should research before you buy, especially because a single drawer can run $800 or more, compared with $200 for a basic full-size dishwasher.

Dishwasher drawers are 24 inches wide and 22 inches deep, the same as a standard dishwasher. Where you save space is with the height of the unit. A single drawer is 17 inches, half the height of a standard dishwasher.

A double-drawer unit is about the same size as a regular dishwasher, but the drawers can be operated individually. While one is full of dirty dishes, you can store clean dishes in the other.

Ask yourself if a single drawer alone is big enough to handle what your clan dishes out. A drawer holds fewer items than a standard dishwasher, so if you have a family of four or more or have lots of parties, you may need both a regular model and a drawer.

(Continued)

■ Fast Facts on Dishwasher Drawers (*Continued*)

Ask if the racks are adjustable so you can load oversized items, such as a saute pan, or delicates, such as fluted champagne glasses. Look for foldable shelves and compartments for smaller items, such as baby utensils.

How quiet is the dishwasher? With dishwashers, noise is measured in sones, which is a unit of perceived loudness. Some are so quiet they have "end of cycle beeps," to let you know when the load is finished.

Dishwashers are part of the Environmental Protection Agency's ENERGY STAR program, but the smaller drawer models won't have their own efficiency standards for electrical use until 2007.

There are two energy-use issues to consider: 1) How does the water reach the proper temperature for sterilizing dishes and utensils? 2) If it can accomplish this at the same temperature your water heater provides, you'll use less energy than if the dishwasher has a booster heater. On the other hand, because a final rinse usually requires a temperature of 160 degrees or better, a dishwasher with an internal heating element will be less expensive to buy and safer to operate than trying to get your home water heater up to that required temperature.

How much water does it take to do a full load of dishes? Some drawer models use less than two gallons per load. (Some models won't start if they're overloaded, especially because the spray pattern needed to wash the dishes can be blocked. Others may have built-in flooding protection.)

Most drawer models come with the same features high-end, standard-size dishwashers have. There are delicate cycles for washing crystal and fine china at lower pressures; heavy-duty settings for pots and pans or for removing caked-on eggs; and different drying cycles, or the option of forgoing the drying cycle and letting dishes air-dry to save energy.

A timer or delay cycle is useful for setting the dishwasher to run at a specific time. It also helps balance appliance energy use and prevents dishwasher noise during certain hours.

Some models offer indicator lights for when the rinse liquid gets too low, and some models come with readouts showing time remaining until the dishes are done.

Stainless steel interiors last the longest, although plastic ones have 20-year guarantees. Make sure you read and discuss with the dealer the service and manufacturer's warranties, and make sure someone qualified to deal with dishwasher drawers is readily available.

Single-drawer dishwashers range from $800 to $1,200; double drawers start at $1,300 and go as high as $2,000.

If a dishwasher drawer still proves to be too big for your kitchen, or too expensive, a compact dishwasher, which is about the size of a large countertop microwave oven, might be the answer. Or, a portable dishwasher that rolls up to the sink and hooks up to the waterline, but can be stored in a closet, might work for you.

Full-size dishwashers range in price from $300 to $1,750. Installation can run from $150 to $300, depending on the amount of plumbing and electrical work required.

A modern city condo kitchen has an unusual center island.

■ THE KITCHEN SINK

Even if it does take longer to wash dishes by hand, the sink and faucets you choose are critical to the successful operation of the kitchen. Stainless steel seems to be the most popular choice, even though the steel should be thick enough to avoid denting if a big pot is dropped full force on the surface. Porcelain looks nice but can chip easily; solid-surface materials, which are the priciest, can be easily scratched; and acrylics don't stand up to heat all that well. Sinks can be top mounted (the lip sits on the edge of the opening) or bottom mounted (the sink looks as if it is part of the countertop), which is easier to clean if you can just sweep the crumbs and vegetable matter into the sink unobstructed.

There are single-bowl sinks and double-bowl ones, with the garbage disposal fitting underneath. Sinks are typically 22 or 24 inches wide, 20 inches from front to back and 8 inches deep, although deep-bowl sinks about 9 inches in depth are highly useful for not only filling big pots with water but scrubbing them when they come back dirty from the stove. (The usefulness is enhanced by the use of a gooseneck faucet under which even lobster-cooking pots can be filled.) Prices of sinks range from under $100 for a single-bowl, stainless steel sink to $1,500 for a double-bowl, vitreous china, 35½-inch-wide model. Copper sinks

A designer vent hood made of stainless steel.

Retro style appliances from Elmira Stove Co.

Adding color presents an opportunity for kitchen decor to be eclectic. A designer and client might choose a stainless steel range but also decide to go with red wall ovens. That said, Aga, the British range manufacturer, is selling a chocolate-colored range with four ovens. Price: $5,000 to $20,000, depending on the model.

can cost as much as $5,000. Faucets range from $60 to $1,200 or more, depending on the finish.

■ CABINETS AND COUNTERS

If there haven't been enough options so far—flooring choices are in chapter 15—it is time to tackle the largest kitchen remodeling expenses: cabinets and countertops. Cabinets typically account for 30 to 40 percent of the cost of both new and remodeled kitchens, and despite the outlay, kitchen designers insist that no matter what style of cabinet homeowners choose, most end up being dissatisfied with the choice.

Cabinet price is determined by construction and materials. Consider the cabinet just a box. As a box, it isn't that expensive to make, but then you have to consider what the box is made of; how the box is made; how big the box is; what kind of door closes the box; what kind of trim, finish, and hardware the box and its door have; the composition and construction of the drawers that fit into the box; and the cost of installation of the box so it works properly, or at least opens and closes.

Building industry experts have estimated that, in a new house with a median price of $250,000, 30 linear feet of cabinets costs about $5,500. Unfinished wood cabinets cost about $85 a linear foot, while standard wood finished cabinets are in the $150 to $200 range—both uninstalled. As Americans' need for storage has increased, so have cabinet sizes.

Standard cabinets are 30 inches, but you can get more storage space in ones that are

Stainless steel appliances blend with traditional cabinetry.

Quartz kitchen countertops.

 More Do-It-Yourself Tips Online! **Analyze the electrical needs for your updated kitchen at www.remodelingonthemoney.com**

36 inches or 42 inches high. Typically, if 30-inch cabinets for a kitchen job cost $5,500, increasing the size to 42 inches probably will add $800 to the price.

Oak, maple, and cherry are traditional materials that survive trends. Today's most popular styles for the built-in kitchen are light woods, both in raised-panel and single-slab doors. One of the benefits of light woods is that you can change the style quite easily from more traditional to modern simply by changing the handle and knob options and external accessories. Light woods work well with a wide range of appliances, from classic color choices to stainless steel, which remains a big trend in appliance finishes. Glass doors were popular in the 1990s, until homeowners realized the glass doors allowed visitors to see the clutter better. White kitchen cabinets seem to go in and out of style every year. Cabinet hardware has become an expression of the homeowners' personality. Every knob and drawer pull is a little different, with one a spoon, another a knife, and a third a fork. And there are an increasing number of mom-and-pop manufacturers springing up to produce individualized hardware.

With new cabinets so expensive, there are alternatives. One is refacing, which uses veneer to cover the exposed faces of frames, and new plywood or door panels to cover end panels. New doors, drawer fronts, and moldings are added, as well as new hardware. The cost of refacing tends to be all over the map, depending on the job. Though some consumers complain that refacing can cost as much as buying new cabinets, it is difficult to understand why because you already have the boxes. As with any project, the price for a cabinet refacing will be determined, in part, by the quality of materials selected.

Another is painting the cabinet doors, and that is the route that Ellen Shimberg took when she decided to spruce up her kitchen. The decision on color

Miele's electric cooktop produces consistent heat (Photo courtesy of Miele).

A stainless steel glass door lets you see all the available drinks.

■ Fast Facts on Painting Cabinets

Remove the doors from the cabinets, then remove all the hardware.

Wipe all surfaces with a clean rag saturated with mineral spirits (paint thinner) to remove surface contamination. You may have to do this two or more times because older cabinets typically have a heavy buildup of dirt, grease, or grime and wax. Change the rags frequently to avoid depositing dirt and grease back on the cabinets.

Wash the surface with equal parts household ammonia and water. Rinse well with clean water. Allow the surface to dry completely.

Prime the surface with a shellac-based primer-sealer. Let it dry for about an hour.

The finish coats should be an oil-based paint—alkyd enamel—for a harder, more stain-resistant, washable, and durable finish. Two coats should be enough, but the number of coats depends on the kind of look you want.

Depending on the temperature and the humidity when you are working, each coat may take two or more days to dry. Make sure each coat dries completely and is not tacky to the touch.

Sand the surface with a fine-grit sandpaper to make the coat of paint even and blotch free.

Use a tack cloth to remove all the sanding dust from the surface, and apply the next coat.

It can take a couple of days for a coat to cure, and the time elapsing between coats can make the job last a week. For a better finish, make sure you sand between coats.

---

took a while because visitors were asked their opinions of some color choices Ellen had dabbed on the cabinets.

The numerous decisions involved in choosing cabinets are matched by the number of kitchen countertop options. Once there was just Formica for the masses and granite or marble for the well-to-do, but now there are too many to keep track of and more arriving at the home center every day.

Here are a variety of countertop choices, in no particular order (all prices installed):

Measure for a new countertop by determining the distance from the edges of the countertop to the edges of the sink trim. Transfer those onto a diagram so you can have the sink cutout precut when buying the countertop.

Granite. This type of countertop is expensive, although there are deals available on the Internet if you do your research. It comes in a variety of colors and holds up to heat. It needs to be sealed periodically, absorbs stains, and can crack. Scratches are difficult to remove and unusual sizes and shapes have visible seams. Cost: $50 to $100 a square foot.

Marble. Because of its expense, marble is often used in small areas of the kitchen. It requires constant maintenance and stains easily but is waterproof and heatproof. Like granite, it can scratch and is porous. Cost: $50 to $100 a square foot.

Stainless steel. This looks commercial and, in combination with stainless steel appliances, can overwhelm a kitchen. It clangs when you strike it and can dent. Cost: $150 to $200 a square foot.

Laminate. This type of countertop (Formica and Wilsonart) is inexpensive, durable, comes in lots of colors, and can be installed by do-it-yourselfers. It doesn't stand up to heat, seams show, the end seams are fairly obvious, the colors tend to fade, and chips and cracks cannot be repaired. Cost: $20 to $30 a square foot.

Solid surface. These countertops—Corian and Swanstone, among others—come in a variety of colors but are susceptible to heat and stains. Cost: $55 to $75 a square foot.

Engineered stone. Examples of engineered stone include Silestone and DuPont Zodiaq. This type of countertop has nonporous surfaces, resists scratches, comes in a vast array of colors, and requires no sealing. Cost: $50 to $100 a square foot.

Ceramic tile. This comes in a variety of colors, sizes, and styles; is easy to clean, and can take a hot pan; but the surface is uneven, can chip or crack; and the grout lines stain easily. Cost: $15 to $35 a square foot.

Wood. Wood countertops, including butcher block and bamboo, can be sanded and stained but can be damaged by water and stains over times. Cost: $50 to $100 a square foot.

Concrete. Concrete resists scratches and heat, can be tinted in a variety of colors, and, even though the material is porous, additives and sealants can reduce it, and it can be made into unusual shapes. It can crack, however. Cost: $125 a square foot.

A lot of money is being spent on kitchens, and the experts are often puzzled why someone will go into debt to create space for merely heating up yesterday's leftover takeout. The motivation to remodel has less to do with the kitchen as a place to cook and eat than it does to create a center of the universe for the American family. Kitchens are not just kitchens, but the focal point for busy lives. That alone makes them worth the money.

Following the Master Plan

❝It's as if someone built a house around a small condo.❞

—Gary Schaal, veteran new-home builder

3

In the new-home market, or at least among designers in that market, the words "master suite" and "retreat" are interchangeable. "Fortress" might be a better word than "retreat" because, except maybe for a place to put the car, most master suites, at least in the minds of these designers, are self-contained units that often take up one-quarter of the total area of a typical 2,400-square-foot house, a fact that led Gary Schaal to compare the master suite to a condo. In the 1980s, when the trend to giant-size master suites began, the square footage sacrificed for the space came out of hallways and children's rooms. These days, as children's rooms are smaller versions of what the parents are getting, the required space is being made up by reducing the size of living rooms and dining rooms.

Master suites play a role, although not an overwhelmingly large one, in the remodeling of existing homes. Data show that existing-home renovations focus more on kitchens, bathrooms, and special-function rooms than on master suites. Because the master suite remodel in an existing home is modeled on the ones being created in new-home construction, the amount of square footage needed cannot be carved out of an existing footprint, but requires a substantial addition.

> Master suites have been getting larger because house size has been increasing. Since 1960, the size of a single-family house has grown to 2,400 square feet from 1,100, according to the National Association of Home Builders.

A sitting room with a window seat.

Double pedestal sinks in the master bath.

That is probably the reason why *Remodeling* magazine, in its annual Cost vs. Value survey of popular renovation projects, puts a midrange master suite addition at $73,370, while an upscale master suite project costs almost $138,000. Both projects involve changes to the first floor—including access from the outside through French doors—reflecting the growing trend of bringing the master suite down from the second floor.

Sometimes you have to take what you get and continually reconfigure the interior space to suit evolving needs. Liz and Mike live in a house that Mike bought before they were married, and the previous owner, who had built the house, provided the traditional definition of a master suite, which can accommodate a large bed and a dedicated bathroom, with some closet space. For a few years, it met their needs adequately because they had a lot of room to move around in the rest of the house in case things became too claustrophobic and, because of work and an active social life, the house, rather than the master suite, was their retreat if they needed it.

Whirlpool's Personal Valet is a hot button among consumers. Typically kept in the master-bedroom closet, it cleans and sanitizes clothing in 30 minutes, smoothing wrinkles and removing odors from garments using a water-based formula that revitalizes clothes when activated. Price: $799 to $999.

Then the twins arrived, followed a year later by their brother, and now, three years later, even the master suite has been taken over by kids' stuff. Their bed often doubles as a changing table if the real one is occupied. And while both work full-time, remain active, and all three children spend part of the day in child care, the idea of the master bedroom as a retreat makes them laugh.

> The master suite is the most private of the "privacy components" of the house—a grouping that includes the guest suite and the den/library.

"If we make a change, it will be to increase the size of the kitchen," Liz said. "It probably won't come soon, either, because can you imagine a contractor working around three toddlers who are at the 'No, I won't get out of the way of the power-nailer' stage?"

Tom and Helen, too, would rather spend their money on a bigger, more modern kitchen than a master suite, but they were fortunate that the investors who had remodeled their 1,800-square-foot house had carved out a master suite in the converted attic of their 1½-story Arts and Crafts–style house. It's a perfectly adequate space for their needs and is truly a retreat since Tom turned the basement into a combination bedroom/bathroom for three of their four boys, who are under 10. The youngest boy, who is not yet one year old, sleeps in the master but in an alcove that is off the master bathroom.

Renovation begins on a master suite in a 1930s-era house.

"The only problem with the master suite is that the remodeling didn't include a bump-up of the attic into a full story," Helen said. "That means that the insulation is inadequate, and in the summer, we have two window air conditioners running almost full-time, and we need to operate a small electric heater in the winter for added warmth."

A master suite was part of the two-story addition that Mark and Julia had built a few years back, and the idea of a retreat did play a role in the plans the two teachers had for their house. Yet the baby girl, who arrived after the addition was completed, spent her first three months in the master suite so Julia could get to her quickly during the night so as not to disturb the other two children.

Color is the key to successful master suite design.

Sitting rooms in master suites can be almost
as large as the bedroom itself.

Retreat for Mark didn't mean extravagance (the second-floor master suite
is above an expanded family room they needed to accommodate their growing family), but having their own bathroom meant that they could get ready
for work each morning without having to stand in line with the kids, and that
Julia could keep her makeup out safely on the double-bowl vanity without her
daughters having access to it for "experimentation." There is a computer desk
in the room for accessing email and paying bills, an exercise bike, and a television set, which plays a huge role in the "retreat" aspect of the couple's master
bedroom.

"We come up here to watch television after the kids go to bed," Julia said.

Some adults can live forever without a master suite. Denise and Lane
have made do for more than 30 years sharing a bathroom with two sons. They didn't even con-
sider having a three-by-five-foot bathroom for four people all that much of problem, and only undertook a midrange renovation project when one of the boys had left home and the other was in college. When the boys were little, the master bedroom was not a retreat but a family gathering place. Denise refused to have a television set any-where else in the house and restricted watching to only a few, well-chosen programs a week. The family watched television together, all sitting on the bed or the floor of the master bedroom.

Need to press your dress or pants before
heading to dinner? Broan-NuTone's
PressRite ironing center fits easily in the
master bedroom behind a traditional-
style cabinet door (a separate item) that
hides the ironing board when not in
use. The heavy-gauge 12-by-42-inch
ironing board swivels 180 degrees for
flexibility. The center is prewired for
an iron outlet. The ironing center costs
about $250; custom doors, $75 to $85.

Even the boys shared a room for most of the time they were growing up. Lane built them a bunk bed that incorporated desk space and a toy area that looked like a play fort. When the boys grew to an age where separate rooms were needed, Denise, an artist and wallpaper designer, moved her studio out of the house so that could happen.

■ THE MASTER BATH

A major component of this trend toward increased privacy has been the evolution of the master bath. In the 1960s, when the typical master suite was about 200 square feet, the master bathroom was no more than 6-feet wide. It contained a shower, sink, and regular-size tub. Now the bathroom is a "grooming center," with a soaking tub, double shower with massage jets on "towers," and double vanity sinks with a makeup area in between the two. Master baths have been growing proportionately, taking up as much as 40 percent of the master suite. Whirlpools also are a hot item—a standard feature of new houses, of course, though owners of existing houses are expanding bathrooms to incorporate whirlpools or replacing bathtubs with whirlpools that fit into the space.

There is a trend toward privacy in the toilet area, resulting in creation of a compartmentalized toilet. It helps when two people are using the master bath at the same time, providing some opportunity for modesty. In case the toilet user forgets and flushes while the shower is in use, showers have antiscald faucet devices (usually required by building code). While you are at it, have the scald guards installed on the sink and tub faucets as well.

There are a couple of things to consider when enclosing a toilet. One is that the recommended space for such an enclosure is 36 inches by at the least 66 inches, and that includes a door that opens out to the bathroom. A pocket door is an ideal choice under these circumstances. The other is that some building codes require that toilets be centered 15 inches from the walls and the tub, with 21 inches of clearance in front.

The master bath mirrors what the typical consumer is incorporating into the high-end bathroom renovation project discussed in detail

> Toilet-paper holders should be about 26 inches above the floor, toward the front of the bowl. If you are tired of dealing with spring-loaded holders, a number of manufacturers are making more decorative and stylish versions on which the rolls easily slide on and off and that can be adjusted for use by people with physical disabilities.

Double bowl sinks in the master suite.

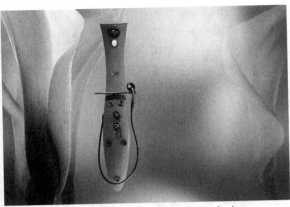

A multispray shower adds pizzazz to a master bathroom.

Focus groups recommend that counters in the master bath be 36 inches off the floor rather than 32 inches because the lower counters mean that the users will have to bend more. Higher counters can accommodate deeper vanity drawers, however. On the other hand, these focus-group recommendations are counter to the principles of universal design for aging in place—30 or 32 inches so that someone in a wheelchair can have access to the sink and turn the faucets on and off.

Ideas for bathroom renovations come from decorating magazines, especially among women. The Internet also is becoming more important as a source for checking out designs and fixtures.

in chapter 1. The difference is that a master bath usually has two of everything, as well as a double shower and a whirlpool, and it is much larger—typically the size of a secondary bedroom. The shower stalls often are made of stone instead of tile, and most have seats that allow the woman of the house a place to shave her legs. Although whirlpools are targeted to women, MTI Whirlpools has debuted one for men, the Isis air tub, for about $3,500. Many women have opted for soaking tubs without jets rather than whirlpools with them.

If you're looking for a sink that will make some sort of statement, vessels seem to be the stuff of which high-end design is made. Though they account for only about 20 percent of the bathroom sink market, they are being produced in an ever-increasing array of styles, shapes, and materials.

There are two sides to vessels—an artistic side and a practical side. Instead of matched and coordinated fixtures, you have a collection, for example, a Mozambique wood stand

■ Fast Facts on Whirlpools

There are whirlpools and there are air jet tubs. The bubbling in an air jet tub is created by air being pushed through several dozen tiny holes. In a whirlpool tub, air and water is forced through several large jets, creating a massage effect. The pressure and flow of the jets are readily adjustable by the bather. Whirlpool tubs come with anywhere from four to eight large jets, and some have smaller jets placed so they can massage the back of the bather's neck or the feet.

The best thing about the modern tub—whirlpool, air jet, or plain-vanilla bath—is that they come in so many shapes and sizes that they can be installed in the tightest and oddest of spaces with relative ease. If the space the old tub occupied is six feet, there is a six-foot-long whirlpool to replace it. Tubs that are recess mounted fit between the walls, which butt against the lip or rim. There are corner tubs and whirlpools that fit into platform with a tile surround.

Typical whirlpools range from 25 to 150 gallons, so the water heater has to have a large enough reservoir to fill the tub with warm water two-thirds of the way. If you have a large-capacity tub, you may want to enlarge your present heater, dedicate a heater to the tub, or add an on-demand or tankless gas or electric water heater to the master suite just for the whirlpool.

As recommended for regular tubs in the chapter on bathrooms, you'll need to try out the whirlpool in the showroom to see if it fits you and you it. Manufacturers suggest that a good size for people both short and tall is about 5½ feet by 36 to 42 inches. As with hot tubs, there is no guarantee that just because you have a whirlpool, you'll use it regularly, so don't buy more than you need, and don't pick a tub for two for the same reason.

Again, as with regular tubs, whirlpools and air jet tubs come in a variety of materials and finishes. Enameled cast iron is durable but heavy and may require additional under-the-floor support, so check things out first with a structural engineer. Molded acrylic tubs resist stains better than fiberglass tubs that are coated with gel, while enameled steel tubs, while probably the most durable, don't come in as many shapes as others.

Access panels should be provided for electrical, plumbing, and heating, ventilation, and air-conditioning (HVAC) systems, and that is also the case for whirlpool and air jet tub maintenance. You may need to be able to reach the pipes of the whirlpool while access to the air jet motor is just about all you'll

A soaking tub makes the master bath a retreat.

(Continued)

■ **Fast Facts on Whirlpools (*Continued*)**

need. Code requires that whirlpool motors have to be powered by dedicated ground fault circuit interrupters (GFCIs). You may prefer a self-cleaning system because these tubs are maintenance-intensive, especially because whirlpools need frequent cleaning because they recirculate water. Some air jet systems purge themselves regularly to remove gunk that will feed bacteria, and because they don't recirculate water, users can add bath oils or salts.

---

on which sits a work of art. The price of art is high. Vitraform introduced the Cubetto, a mouth-blown crystal pedestal with a crystal laminated glass basin and countertop, for a cost of around $9,800. It was shown with a Dornbracht MEM wall-mount faucet that retails for close to $1,000. That's not saying that you can't find a vessel sink for a few hundred dollars. They range in price from mass-produced models starting at $200 to custom-designed vessels that can cost $5,000 or more.

A couple of years back, a fixture manufacturer decided to push the idea that a growing number of homeowners were having urinals installed in new and renovated master baths. While there was no overwhelming evidence to support such a claim, there is enough evidence to suggest that as more money is being spent on master suites, the bidet is making deep inroads into the U.S. market.

The higher-end master suites also have saunas. The

A conventional fireplace in a sitting room of a master suite.

A master suite has plenty of natural light and window seats.

most efficient ones appear to be about 5 feet by 6 feet, and barely clear 7 feet in height, which designers say is ideal for conserving heat and energy. The temperature is about 85 degrees at the sauna floor, 100 degrees at the lower bench, 145 degrees at the upper bench, and 195 degrees at ceiling height. Sauna doors should have no lock and are only 24-inches wide to prevent heat loss. Because the sauna opens pores and flushes out the body's impurities, you have to use soap and water to rinse off the waste. That means you need a shower nearby. You also need a lower vent to allow fresh air through the sauna heater and an upper exhaust vent. Sauna heaters typically are wall-mounted or sit on the floor. The top has peridotite stones that are heated by an electrical element from below. Steam is created by scooping water onto the heated stones. A floor drain is required.

■ WORKING OUT AT HOME

Aging baby boomers are perpetually looking for ways to keep young and fit, but often don't have the hour or so each morning before work to make it to the fitness center. City dwellers have the luxury of walking to and from work, and this kind of low-impact workout does wonders for keeping arthritic knees limber. The vast majority of suburbanites don't have long stretches of sidewalk at their service, so finding a way to exercise at home when there is time available becomes a major consideration in planning the contents of a master suite. Experts say that an area of 10 feet by 10 feet, give or take a foot, is just right to accommodate a couple pieces of exercise equipment. The question is whether that space will

Towel warmers are fast becoming a feature of high-end master bathrooms. While there are a variety of manufacturers, they all work the same way: The warmer, which looks like a radiator, mounts on the wall and can either be plugged in or hard-wired. Myson sells 126 models, 6 finishes, and 1,200 custom colors, so it is highly unlikely that you won't find one that you want if you are so inclined. Even if you don't, Myson will design one for you if you provide the specifications. Some of the warmers are electric and some hydronic, meaning that you can have your plumber hook it into your water-heating system much as you would a radiator. Unlike a radiator, however, putting a wet towel on the warmer won't result in rust deposits. There also are multitowel racks, and the warmer comes with a five-year warranty. Price: $1,400 to $6,000.

Some master suites have bar sinks, under-the-counter refrigerators, coffee-makers, and microwaves so that the occupants don't even have to stop by the kitchen before going to work.

New code requirements mandate that every bathroom have at least one permanent light fixture controlled by a light switch, and wall switches have to be located at least five feet from showers and tub.

be used often enough to justify adding $12,000 (not including the equipment) to the cost of your master suite renovation.

A vessel sink is another way to make a statement in the master suite.

Rough plumbing in a wall of master suite remodeling.

■ Fast Facts About Bidets

The user sits astride the bowl facing the faucet to control the spray or fill the bowl with water. Usually made from vitreous china, it is styled to resemble the shape of the toilet. The bidet is placed next to the toilet in the bathroom, an arrangement meant to encourage personal hygiene.

There are five basic types of bidets:

Over the rim, which is fitted with a standard faucet. The bowl is filled with water the same way you fill a sink. This is generally the cheapest and simplest type to install. Having a rimless bowl makes it easy to clean.

Heated or flushing rim, which has hot/cold handles on top, but the water enters the bowl below the rim of the basin.

The spray, which provides a gentle shower and comes in two versions: the vertical, which has a fountain jet in the center of the bowl, and the horizontal, which has a special over-the-rim spout that delivers a horizontal stream of water.

The combination, which offers the heated rim and a vertical spray option in one unit.

The standard bidet is mounted to the floor and is about 15 inches high. The drain trap and supply lines can be brought in from the wall or the floor.

Old framing is cut away to make room for the new.

Consider making the exercise space flexible for other uses if you decide that running with your MP3 player for a mile every day is preferable to walking on a treadmill for an hour and never getting anywhere. Some fitness experts suggest that the home exercise room mirror the fitness center setups by actually having a wall of mirrors to keep track of your progress toward "buffness." While some people might consider a wall of mirrors hard to work around if the exercise room is remodeled into something else, such a wall is perfect to incorporate into an expanded walk-in closet.

Exercise can cause vibrations and create considerable noise. If you want to incorporate an exercise room into the master suite space, whether it is on the first floor or higher up in the house, employ a structural engineer to determine the soundness of the joists to minimize or eliminate shaking. Noise issues can be handled by soundproofing insulation manufactured by Owens Corning and others. Carpet (loose fibers can get into the machine), hardwood (damage to the floor), or concrete floors (hard on the exerciser and painful if you fall on them) are unsuitable. Instead, put all the equipment on a rubber mat or rubber click-together flooring that will absorb

No matter where you put your exercise room, make sure there is at least eight or nine feet of clearance above the floor. A lot of exercise machines are as tall as seven feet, and even if your equipment is short, an exuberant jumping jack might cause you to hit the ceiling.

impact, reduce noise and vibration, clean quickly and easily, and won't retain perspiration odor. Don't forget the placement of the television set—just so you won't get bored. Some exercise machines come with an eye-level attachment that will hold a book.

If you don't have enough space for a whole exercise area, there are a few pieces of equipment to consider if you're determined to turn some of those extra pounds into muscle mass. Most are designed to fit into small spaces, the kind frequently found in basements and bedrooms.

A light switch is controlled by motion.

■ STORAGE

Never, never, never remodel a master suite without increasing the storage space. This is something that homebuilders have long known, yet they realize that the demand for storage always exceeds what they provide, according to builder Gary Schaal, who explains that "buyers say that there's never enough, even though the amount and variety of storage space has been increasing for at least the past 15 years. The closets are never big enough, even if they are his-and-hers walk-ins in the master bedroom, because it seems that the woman wants more storage space than the man. We are even including walk-in closets in children's rooms."

Framing out the master bedroom door.

Remodeler Jay Cipriani says that, in existing homes, "the question always is how to pick up extra storage space without breaking the budget, or at least spending a reasonable amount to obtain it. We have this conversation no matter what we are building—a bathroom, a kitchen, or a two-story addition. The solution: If we are doing a cathedral ceiling, we can add a loft. If we are building an addition and are putting

A fireplace is the focal point of a master bedroom.

it on top of a three-foot crawlspace, we can dig down another five feet and add a full basement for $5,000 to $6,000 more. If a crawlspace is the only answer, we can install a French-drain system to guarantee dry storage, even if you pack the place from top to bottom."

Alternatives include pull-down steps and plywood floors for attic storage, tearing out old soffits in kitchens to change 30-inch cabinets to 42-inchers, hanging cabinets over toilets and washers and dryers, and adding organizing systems to existing closets and storage lofts to garages.

Heat N Glo's Cyclone provides heat and focus to a sitting room in a master suite (Photo courtesy of Heat 'N' Glo.).

(Left) Walk-in closets shared by both requires organization.

■ Fast Facts on Designing a Master Suite Closet

Even if you do get rid of your clothes, it has to be a walk-in closet and, in most cases, it has to provide enough storage for the present and future needs of two people.

Size does matter. You have a couple of options in a walk-in, with one being 8 feet by 6 feet by 8 feet and the larger one at 10 feet by 10 feet by 10 feet.

You have plenty of material choices such as wood and metal or a metallic finish, which are the most common. You need to figure out how many drawers you'll need and how much space is required for your shoes.

How much space do you need for storing long garments such as coats and dresses? Do you need lots of room for storage boxes, sweaters, sweatshirts, and other clothing that is usually stored folded?

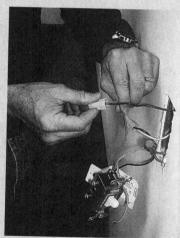

A regular light switch is converted to a motion sensitive one.

How high do you want the storage to be? Can clothing and other items that you don't use regularly be stacked to the ceiling?

More Do-It-Yourself Tips Online!

Looking for the best storage system fit for the space you have? Ideas abound at www.remodelingonthemoney.com

When you are considering the storage needs for your master suite renovation, consider first getting rid of the stuff that you don't really need. Clutter is the result of people losing control of things and is created by busy lives. You work long hours, and then you come home and don't really want to clean the closets and cabinets, so you just dump stuff on available flat surfaces. That's why no one is eating at a lot of dining room tables.

By the time most people have reached their 40s and 50s, they have been collecting stuff without pause for more than 20 years. Garages hold a collection of bikes and lawn equipment instead of cars. Closets have clothes that their owners could wear again if only they could lose 10 pounds. Shoes are waiting to come back into style.

■ ADDING WARMTH TO YOUR MASTER SUITE

Looking for a way to add romance to the master suite? Consider a gas fireplace. The fireplace has been standard in new construction for at least 15 years, if not more. What has changed is not the size of the fireplace, but the number of fireplaces and their locations. The shift from masonry to prefab designer boxes has put fireplaces in bathrooms, dining rooms, and bedrooms. Fireplaces can be seen on walls of entertainment rooms and below big-screen televisions so that you have your choice of what you want to see.

Designer fireplaces in this case include two-sided glass models located in the pass-through from the master bedroom to the sitting room. The increase in locations results from advances in technology, such as the development of gas fireplaces and the ability to vent them through a wall to the outside without a masonry chimney and the use of flexible pipe for bringing the gas to the units.

Vent-free fireplaces also are an option, although the main issue, despite arguments to the contrary from trade groups promoting them, is safety. There has to be a constant supply of fresh air in the house to guarantee safe operation. All of these units, however, have both a carbon monoxide monitor and an oxygen-depletion sensor. If the level of oxygen in the room with the fireplace reaches a dangerous level, the flame shuts off immediately.

Wariness about vent-free appliances persists, and the units are banned in some states. Both unvented and vented heating appliances must be properly maintained to reduce the risk for associated health hazards. Electric fireplaces are making some inroads into the market, although the amount of radiant heat that plug-in fireplaces provide still remains well below the 15,000 to 40,000 BTUs (British thermal units) that gas fireplaces generate.

The typical cost of a standard gas fireplace is $600 to $3,000, without installation. Electric fireplaces run about $1,200 to $1,500, but usually generate enough heat to take the edge off one or two rooms.

Rick and Amy have problems heating and cooling their master suite, and one suggestion, at least for boosting warmth, is to consider radiant floor heating. This technique has been around since Roman times, and has increased in popularity thanks to exposure on the how-to television shows.

What has made radiant floor heating possible on upper floors of a house was the invention of PEX, a flexible polyethylene tubing that requires fewer fittings and joints than traditional copper pipe. That means the potential for leaks is less because leaks tend to occur at joints. It isn't prone to corrosion, and it is typically laid out in one continuous length of plastic piping. Instead of being embedded in heavy concrete as copper or cast-iron pipes required, PEX is laid in a lightweight, plasterlike material.

> Brighter colors will make the master bedroom look more spacious. The number of spaces in a master suite offers the homeowner the option to use any number of paint colors and finishes.

In a radiant floor or hydronic heating system, heated water circulating through plastic tubes under the floor behaves just like a radiator, transferring heat uniformly from the floor to the objects above it. Unlike forced-air systems, the heat doesn't rise but remains where it is needed, heating the living space. As a result, the temperature near the ceiling, where warm air tends to rise, is often several degrees cooler than the temperature six feet above the floor.

The warm water in a radiant floor system can be generated by a hot water heater or existing hydronic equipment such as a hot water baseboard or radiator. It also can come from a new gas- or oil-fired boiler. Energy savings generated by the system, which proponents say is typically 30 percent, is achieved by not having to heat the water any more than 85 to 95 degrees.

With proper design, radiant floor heating means that the house can be kept at a constant 66 degrees. That would be the same as keeping the thermostat in a forced-air system at 72 degrees. To maintain the consistent temperature requires the use of an indoor-outdoor boiler-reset control. An outdoor thermostat senses the outside air temperature. The indoor thermostat monitors the temperature of the circulating water in the floor. Those two temperatures are fed into

> Every time the temperature outdoors drops 10 degrees, there is a corresponding 10-degree increase in the temperature of the circulating water. It is like the cruise control in a car. There is enough heat to compensate for the difference, but no more.

a computer that varies the speed of the pump injecting the water from the boiler into the tubing.

The price of installing a system that provides 100 percent of the heat for a 2,000-square-foot house can range from $25,000 to $50,000, depending on the number of zones, the sophistication of controls, mixing technology, and heat source; a boiler can range from $2,000 to $12,000. If a system is used in only parts of the house and combined with hot water baseboard heat, the installation cost can be as low as $2,500. That arrangement is more typical, with two heating zones rather than eight.

It is expensive, but advocates of energy-efficient construction suggest that with proper insulation and ventilation, radiant floor heating will save money in the long term. If you are spending several thousand dollars on a master suite renovation, anywhere you can get money back is a good thing.

In addition, getting out of bed on a cold winter morning will be less of a shock with radiant floor heating.

Warm feet are happy feet.

No Place Like the Home Office

❝It's an effort to get us to work 24/7.**❞**

—**Bari Shor, real estate agent**

4

A few years back, housing industry experts and others were predicting that the majority of white-collar workers would soon be "telecommuting" to their offices rather than hopping in the car and spending long hours in impossibly heavy traffic driving to and from the office each day.

The prediction has yet to come true. When these experts looked a little more deeply into their data, they discovered that they had forgotten to consider the social implications of telecommuting—the fact that face-to-face contact with coworkers around the coffee machine is more appealing to the typical human being than virtual isolation in what is often a relatively small and uninviting space in the corner of a bedroom or basement.

The home office appears to work most effectively, no matter what it looks like, for people who either operate a business from it or work much farther than 45 minutes from headquarters.

John has carved out space in a spare room on the second floor of his house for an office, but

> If you have a home office and use it exclusively for business, you can deduct many of the costs associated with the office on your federal income tax return. If you do use this deduction, however, income generated by the office might be taxed by the state or the municipality you live in.

> Building industry surveys consistently show that home offices are usually important to those who earn $100,000 and more each year and whose house cost them $250,000 or more.

Wire used for high-speed cable connections.

A more formal home office, minus computer, has more of a traditional look.

admits that he spends a lot of time on airplanes and in the car to visit clients "because personal, face-to-face contact is a more effective tool than email or telephone calls that might not be answered." John also has discovered, as most home workers do, that "business-related materials often are scattered around the house during the course of the workweek, and I'm always trying to locate things I need that I think are in the office but might have been left on the kitchen table."

Mary works for a major corporation, but the corporate offices are either a five-hour car ride or a two-hour plane ride away from her home. Yet for the past several years, she has been able to conduct day-to-day business activities from her home office, including conference calls, because "technology has progressed so much that contact with the outside world is no longer limited to the standard telephone line." That means if she is involved in a conference call with colleagues and needs to find an answer to a question quickly, she can dial her cell phone or click on her computer—which is tied into a high-speed DSL (digital subscriber line) connection provided by her telephone company—and find the answer.

DSL allows you to maintain your Internet connection and still use the telephone for voice calls. Access to the Internet comes at a much higher speed than a phone-line modem. DSL, typically provided by the telephone company, uses existing lines and often comes with a modem thrown in. DSL is not available in all areas, and the farther you are from the phone company's central office, the less reliable it can be. It also receives data faster than it sends it.

While some of this will be discussed in chapter 7 on home automation, the key to the success of a home office is the availability of technology. The home office user is trying to

A home office chair should be ergonomic, comfortable and adjustable.

replicate some of what is available at the corporate headquarters without having to pay an extraordinary amount for it—especially if much of the activity in the office is to complete work that the user wasn't able to tackle during the workday, and the home office is not a deductible expense so the costs have to be borne by the user.

Most residential wiring in homes built before 1990 is what is known as Category 1, and is designed solely for voice communication. Advanced wiring is known as Category 5, which uses four twisted pairs of wires instead of one for high-speed movement of data. The Category 5 wiring is coupled with an upgraded coaxial TV cable that enables video signals to travel to television and computer monitors throughout the house. The cost of such sophisticated wiring has been dropping so rapidly that what once was a $10,000 to $15,000 optional upgrade now adds only $700 to $1,500 to a builder's costs, depending on the square footage of the house. Recent data show that 50 percent of all new construction in the United States now comes with a standard package of this more sophisticated wiring.

It is, of course, much easier to include Category 5 and coaxial wiring in a new house than an existing one because rewiring an old house usually involves breaking through plaster walls at great expense. There are a couple of solutions. If you are embarking on a major renovation, and the walls will be broken into anyway, add the wiring. If you are having substantial electrical service upgrades done, have the electrician fish the advanced wiring through the walls at the same time.

The most viable alternative to expensive rewiring is the wireless router. A wireless router costs as little as $75 and can provide high-speed Internet access to computers up to 150 feet

If you don't meet the IRS home office deduction rules (regular and exclusive use/principal place of business), you can still deduct ordinary and necessary business expenses that you incur at home; for instance, long-distance phone calls, a separate business telephone line, and the cost of office supplies and equipment. The rules apply only to the expenses of actually running and maintaining your home—such as utilities, rent, depreciation, home insurance, mortgage interest, real estate taxes, and repairs.

■ Fast Facts on Advanced Wiring

Advanced wiring systems typically have three main components:

Service center. This is where all outside services enter the house, including cable TV, telephone, and Internet. This central hub distributes the services to locations throughout the house in a way similar to how the electrical breaker panel controls electricity flow.

High-speed performance cables. These are cables that are Category 5, or better twisted-pair cable for phone and data, and RG-6 coaxial for TV and video. Coaxial provides maximum protection from interference with your TV picture. Category 5 provides high-speed access to multiple phone lines without cross-talk.

Outlets. The outlets in each room determine the services available in that room and can be customized to fit your needs.

Every home office computer should have a backup hard drive.

The Ethernet connection to the router.

Buying a printer? Get one that provides more than one function. For about $200, there are multipurpose machines that can print high-quality digital photos, copy, send faxes, and scan photos and documents. One multipurpose machine reduces space needs, uses less energy than separate equipment, and generates less heat.

from the base station, which is connected to a high-speed cable or DSL broadband modem. To be part of the router network, each computer, whether desktop or laptop, must have a wireless card that comes with the PC or can be purchased separately ($50) and plugged into the computer. While some argue that a wireless setup is not as secure as a hardwired Cat 5 one, router access is usually password protected. Depending on the router, many computers can access the Internet at the same time without a noticeable reduction in speed at most times of the day. In some instances, the router will allow all the computers in the house to be networked to a single printer, although some higher-end, multipurpose printers come with wireless cards or Ethernet adapters that can be fitted with a wireless card with a few adjustments.

In most existing houses, finding a spot for the home office is about 90 percent of the battle. In Stan and Sally's case, a spot in the corner of their large kitchen was adequate for their needs because Stan pays for a law office just a few miles from the house and tries to avoid working on family time. Sally, who is a government lawyer, feels the same way. The computer in the corner of the kitchen is there for everyone, including their two children. The flat-screen desktop computer is linked to the Internet by cable modem.

Cable modems compete with DSL for high-speed connectivity. If you subscribe to digital cable services, your cable modem will likely provide top-of-the-line service, no matter how far you are from the cable company office. One problem: The more cable modem subscribers in your immediate vicinity, the greater the competition for broadband on whatever channel the service is being provided. Most cable companies will add broadband channels as the demand increases to maintain the quality of service.

Locating the home office in the kitchen makes sense, especially because kitchens have become the center of the home universe in the past 20 years. When Allison and Scott built an addition that included a new kitchen, they turned the adjacent old kitchen space into a computer room for the family. Most people still pay bills at the kitchen table, and if the children are going to hang around or near the kitchen, it might be a good place for both parents and children to work on various projects. One show house at a recent conference featured what the builders called the "home management center" right off the kitchen. This center had workstations for the children and provided a computer just for monitoring energy use (the house also demonstrated energy efficiency) and home security. Yet the house also had office space in the master suite where a parent could go to do serious work.

Some home offices share space with the guest bedroom, which works well unless one entertains visitors frequently. Because many company employees are bringing work home so they can be close to their families, the office

A recent poll of residential architects showed that 49 percent of their clients were asking that home offices be included in the design of remodeling projects. This made the home office the most popular of all special-purpose rooms being requested (the home theater was a distant second). Main reasons cited included rising gasoline prices and more flexible telecommuting options.

Many architects and designers decline to include an office in the master suite, preferring to see it as a retreat from work rather than a place to do more of it.

is sometimes located intentionally near the children's playroom or the family room so Mom and Dad can pop out whenever they're needed.

That setup didn't quite work for Alex, whose cramped home office was on the other side of the basement playroom wall. Alex, who works for a pharmaceutical company, and is based

This home office isn't a separate room but still can function as one.

A chair attached to a computer desk can save space in a bedroom or guest room.

■ Fast Facts About Why People Work at Home

About 20 million Americans usually do some work at home as part of their primary jobs, according to the Census Bureau. These people, who reported working at home at least once a week, accounted for 15 percent of total employment.

Half of those were wage and salary workers who took work home on an unpaid basis, the Census Bureau reports. An additional 17 percent had a formal arrangement with their employer to be paid for the work they did at home.

The rest, 30 percent, were self-employed.

Wage and salary employees who were expressly paid to work at home worked there 18 hours per week on average; those who were just taking work home from the job usually worked about 7 hours per week at home.

The statistics appear to support anecdotal evidence that although more people are working at home, the work they are doing is what couldn't be finished at the office rather than complete abandonment of the centralized workplace.

in his home when not traveling, needed more space, and, when a two-story addition included an expanded basement, jumped at the chance to increase the size to accommodate more document storage in a larger office. Although there is still family space near the basement office, most of the children's indoor activity is now done in the new family room between the new kitchen and the outdoor deck.

People who operate businesses from their homes, especially those who deal with visitors and clients, will need to put those offices on the first floor, and, if possible, have a separate entrance. Home business offices also operate under a different set of rules than one that serves to handle the overflow of off-premises work, including accessibility issues covered by the *Americans with Disabilities Act*. Many home businesses need special permits from the state and municipal governments to operate, and homeowners' insurance may not cover the business—for example, if a client slips and falls coming through the entrance or in cases of theft of electronic equipment or fire—even if it is in the house.

If you live in an older house where the floor plan is not as open as a newer one, finding adequate space for an office is going to be a struggle, especially if you want enough workspace, light, and storage. While today's new house is running about 2,400 square feet of usable space, houses built between 1945 and 1980 have anywhere between 1,200 and 1,800 square feet. Because a lot of people who work at home part or all of the time do so to help pay the mortgage, there are a lot of budget constraints, and these people aren't willing to go more heavily into debt for a remodel that would add the home office of their dreams.

Creating an island of work in a multi-purpose sea? Consider room dividers that double as bookcases. As part of its home office line, the Swedish furniture maker Ikea makes the Expedit bookcase that serves this double duty for about $180.

Before you put an office in the basement, make absolutely sure that the basement is dry. If there are sump pumps managing the moisture, make sure they are in working order. You also may need to run the dehumidifier constantly, especially in the warmer months, to prevent moisture damage to books, papers, files, and electronic equipment.

In the luxury group, some upscale buyers are demanding two home offices. The New American Home that was built for the 1998 International Builders Show in Dallas featured two rather extravagant home offices for him and her. The rooms were relatively far from one another; the man's office was for business, the woman's was dominated by crafts—an oddity in a two-paycheck society.

A computer cabinet or credenza is a fine piece of furniture and serves the same function as a butler's pantry when you are looking to work with smaller spaces: It provides a workstation where nothing else will suffice. Yet, because a butler's pantry is no substitute for walk-in storage, a credenza doesn't come anywhere near serving home office needs.

When it comes to adding on, there are some options you can consider if you are OK about dipping into whatever equity your house may be stockpiling. Look into an add-on sunroom or enclosed patio. Depending on the amenities, these add-ons start at about $15,000. Another option is the "Ultimate Backyard Office," an easy-to-assemble, panelized cedar building manufactured by Cedarshed Industries, a British Columbia company. Prices start at $12,999.

While the experts suggest that a 10-by-10-foot space is adequate for a home office with a single user at a time, most of us will have to deal with existing space, so the goal is to make that space as functional, efficient, and comfortable as possible, especially if you will be spending long hours at your tasks. Wireless technology has added considerable flexibility to carving out home office space, but it hasn't made furnishings, lighting, and storage any easier. Modular office furniture is one solution to the work surface and storage problems that need to be handled because the furniture can be reconfigured as needs change.

HP's All-in-One multipurpose machine features a fax, copier, scanner and printer for $199, and doesn't take up as much space as having all of those separate machines.

The push for home offices will only increase because baby boomers, never sure whether they have saved enough money for retirement, will work later in life than their parents. Many residents of active adult communities telecommute to part-time or full-time jobs. Even after 65, they continue to work from spaces in their homes.

The experts also say a work surface of five feet is adequate, but because computers haven't transformed us into a paperless society, that surface can be cluttered easily. Some home office users in need of lots of work surface buy a hollow core wood door at the home center and sit it on two sturdy metal file cabinets. Also, try to manage the clutter. Once you're through with files, store them in a place where

Watch the step by step construction of a home office in basement space at www.remodelingonthemoney.com

Inside a CedarShed cedar office; heating and air conditioning can be added easily (Photo courtesy of CedarShed).

you can find them easily. Buy packages of easy-to-assemble file boxes for under $20 and list the contents on a sheet of paper taped to the front of the box so you can easily see it.

Remember to look at all the space available to you in your home office. The floor space may be minimal, but the wall space is there for the taking, if you know how to use it. Bookcases from floor to ceiling, stacked file drawers and cabinets, CD towers—all offer space for storage. Don't feel bad if others consider the space ugly. It's what matters to you that counts for everything.

Do a lot of talking on the telephone? Invest in a telephone headset (Plantronics makes the best and its $89.99 model is just about right for every home office user, even the ones who do long phone interviews. You can always buy a speaker phone, but it can create an echo even in a small space, and both you and the caller can be difficult to understand. Otherwise, you will be opening yourself up to major neck pain by trying to balance the receiver on your shoulder while typing.

One of the keys to home office design involves ergonomics. Depending on the tasks a person is bringing to the work table, he or she can spend hours face-to-face with a computer screen with little ability to move. Consider, too, that computer overuse often leads to the development of painful carpal tunnel syndrome. The two major pieces of the ergonomic puzzle, therefore, are the chair and the height of the computer keyboard. Don't skimp on the chair, which should be on wheels or some sort of rollers and should be completely and easily adjustable, including tilt back, seat height, and arm rests. When you are sitting facing your computer, your knees should be level with your hips so you aren't putting lots of unnecessary pressure on your lower back. You

> Can't keep track of everything and you have too much to track for the average bulletin board? Buy pieces of cork and make your own. Four 12-by-12-inch squares cost about $12 and stick easily to any wall with two-sided adhesive tape. Two packages can provide enough space for your needs.

Buy a chair mat (prices start at $20). These mats, which are made of vinyl, wood, or other smooth materials, sit under the desk and the chair wheels. Those wheels can damage flooring and often cannot move easily over carpet. A chair mat solves both problems.

need to try out the chairs before you buy, much as you would a replacement bathtub.

The same advice applies to the keyboard tray, which should tilt in a way that allows you to keep your wrists straight, rather than bent up or down, and your elbows at a 90-degree angle. The keyboard tray works with a desktop PC and can be used with laptops that could accommodate such keyboards, which too many users balance on their laps for long periods, creating similar kinds of body aches and pains. The solution is to work on a computer table no more than 30 inches high, and to adjust the screen so that you minimize the glare from overhead lights while keeping it at eye level so you don't develop a crick in your neck.

Always back up everything on your computer, even if your computer has the most storage space technologically available. You can always burn that information onto CD-ROMs, but the easiest and least labor-intensive method is by buying and using a backup hard drive. These devices start at 40 gigabytes and cost about $90, but the best advice is to buy more than you ever think you'll need—especially if you take a lot of digital photos—or around 160 to 240 gigabytes.

A wireless broadband router that is password protected carries high-speed cable connections around the house.

(Left) This home office isn't a separate room but still can function as one.

A home office made for two, off the kitchen.

If you've ever lost a computer hard drive to a lightning strike, you recognize the importance of plugging your electronic devices into a surge protector. A surge protector is not to be confused with a power strip of outlets that may or may not be a surge protector. One of the primary differences is price: You can pick up a power strip for about $15, but a surge protector that includes plugs for telephone and cable modems can run four or five times that much. Some of the surge protectors come with insurance policies that will pay damages if the device fails to protect any of the equipment plugged into it. Some protectors don't handle lightning. Make sure the one that you buy does.

Every elementary school child knows the origins of lightning, but it often requires an electrical engineer to explain the reasons for power surges. If, for example, a microwave that is plugged into the same circuit as the computer is started, a small fluctuation in the power can cause the computer screen to flicker just a bit. The older the wiring in the house, the better the

---

■ Fast Facts on Home Office Lighting

Try to arrange the lighting to eliminate computer screen glare, which includes light coming through office windows. You may need to install shades, blinds, or curtains to eliminate or soften direct sunlight during the day. Too much glare can lead to eye problems and headaches.

Lighting is designed to create a work space that is both comfortable and has focused illumination for reading, writing, and computer operation.

There are three forms of lighting: ambient, which illuminates the entire room so someone entering can negotiate it safely (the switch at the door); task, which brightens specific spaces such as desks and bookcase shelves; and accent, which highlights certain features in the room.

Two large ceiling fixtures, placed overhead to the right and left of the desk, can provide effective lighting and reduce shadows. Don't position light fixtures in front of your desk because this may cause reflections.

An adjustable lamp can do a fine job illuminating the keyboard and desk.

Not enough room indoors for a home office? CedarShed has outdoor offices starting at $12,000 (Photo courtesy of CedarShed).

(Left) Bookcases from Ikea set the home office apart from the rest of the basement.

Incandescent lights and inefficient office equipment create substantial waste heat that could make the temperature in your office uncomfortable and increase cooling costs. To avoid this, look for the ENERGY STAR label when choosing computers, monitors, printers, fax machines, copiers, scanners, and multifunction devices.

chance of power variations and surges. Make sure the electrical wiring to the home office is up to snuff. While computers and other office equipment are designed not to consume much juice, other demands on old wiring can cause damage and even result in fire. If you are going to make yourself more comfortable in the space with such amenities as a compact refrigerator, a coffeemaker, or even a small microwave, hire a licensed electrician to upgrade the wiring. If the office is in the basement or another area of high moisture, don't forget to install ground fault interrupter circuit (GFIC) outlets and switches. This work can be done in conjunction with an upgrade of the whole-house electrical service.

While we are dealing with electricity, we should spend some time emphasizing the importance of lighting to home office operations.

If you can work it in and have cable connections in the work space, add a small television set to your home office, such as a 13 inch with a built-in VCR that costs under $100. Although it can often be a distraction, the noise the TV produces can make up for the absence of coffeemaker conversation at the corporate office.

Get Comfortable, Save Money

"People tend to be interested in energy efficiency if it will make their houses more comfortable."

—Hap Haven, energy expert

5

The late Richard Pronnecke, who spent more than 30 years living alone in a cabin in the Alaskan wilderness, once wrote in his diary that thanks to his fireplace and his stove, his cabin was "a toasty 40 degrees." That must have been the first time 40 degrees and toasty ever appeared in the same English sentence. The Inuit language does not have a word for toasty, but one assumes that the word for "shiver"—*olikpok*—would suffice.

Most homeowners would have called the furnace repair person hours before the inside temperature reached that point, so comfort is a matter of perspective. If it is 30 below zero in the Alaskan wilderness, 40 degrees feels comfortable. If you are used to cranking the furnace to 68, 40 degrees is an emergency serious enough to head for a motel until the furnace is repaired.

Until 1973, few middle-class Americans cared about using great quantities of natural gas or fuel oil to overheat their houses in cold weather, because energy was cheap. Then Organization of Petroleum Exporting Countries (OPEC) decided to end the holiday, and energy prices have been fluctuating since. The response by builders was to overinsulate and underventilate houses, lowering energy bills but compromising indoor air quality. President Jimmy Carter put solar panels on the White House roof, which were removed by the Reagan Administration a few years later.

Energy efficiency and green or sustainable building go together. *Building green* means building or renovating houses in such a way that resources are conserved. For example, a builder can employ planning and design techniques that preserve the natural environment and minimize disturbance to the land. It also means reducing waste during renovation or construction and throughout the life of the home.

A lot of people believe that green building is only for new construction, but Clark and Lara bought a townhouse a few years back and decided to prove that an existing structure could become "green" without anyone noticing the differences. Typically, it isn't easy to incorporate green design into a renovation project because you're often working with existing materials and building footprints that cannot readily accommodate the changes such design requires.

A high-efficiency furnace, manufactured by Rheem, is designed to save money by using less fuel.

Before Clark and Lara bought the building, it had housed a first-floor business and apartments on the two upper floors, which meant that it had to be gutted. Still, the interior retains the signature floor plan of the original townhouse. Walk in the front door, and you

Green tip: Choose insulation with a high content of recycled material, including 100 percent recycled paper.

can see through the living room and kitchen to the back garden wall. They kept the commercial facade, but replaced the windows with energy-efficient units.

The couple insulated, replaced stairs, and reworked existing spaces, but they limited their expansion of the footprint of the house to a three-story, steel-framed glass wall in the left corner of the rear wall. The change enhances both passive solar heating and the source of natural light in the winter. The first-floor glass wall opens the kitchen to a postage stamp–size garden, which remains a work in progress.

Clark and Lara looked into a solar alternative to standard air-conditioning, but found that the systems would overwhelm a

Fiberglass insulation cut to fit into framed openings is made completely tight with caulk.

1,680-square-foot house. The trade-off in energy savings comes in solar hot water and the radiant floor heating in the winter.

The solar-heating system cost $11,300 and includes the solar hot water heater and a gas-fired backup in the basement. The two solar collectors on the roof—there's a frame for a third—are composed of a series of glass tubes with a coating that absorbs solar energy well but that inhibits radiative heat loss. Air is removed from the space between the glass tubes and some metal tubes to form a vacuum, which eliminates conductive and convective heat loss.

It's an indirect circulation system, which pumps a mixture of glycol and water antifreeze through collectors. Heat exchangers transfer the heat from the fluid to the drinkable water stored in the tanks. If the glycol gets too hot, the additional heat is returned to radiators on the roof and expelled. The couple coated their rubber roof with a white elastomeric substance that reflects sunlight and thus keeps the roof cooler, and the radiated extra heat is deflected as well.

In the winter, any extra heated water from the solar heater is fed through a heat exchanger to the gas-fired hot water heater that supplies the radiant system. That hot water heater is the primary source for the radiant flooring's heat, which is zoned for each floor. Instead of the 180 degrees needed for a boiler to supply radiators, 110 degrees is all that's needed to make them comfortable in colder weather.

That system cost $11,600 for all three floors. To accommodate the weight of the "lightweight" mixture of gypsum and concrete into which the plastic piping for the system is embedded, the joists on the top two floors had to be reinforced. The "gypcrete" added $2,000 to the total cost of the system.

Heat pumps are considered one of the most highly efficient forms of heating, but they work best in cool, not cold, climates, experts say. In frigid weather, the heat pump might not be able to reach a certain temperature range in a certain time, and supplemental and very expensive electric resistance heating kicks in to help.

President George W. Bush's ranch in Crawford, Texas, features passive solar heating, a heat exchange system using underground water that keeps the interior warm in winter and cool in summer, and a gray-water reclamation system that treats and reuses waste water.

In bright sun, a four-inch-wide photovoltaic cell produces about 1.5 watts of electricity in a year. A solar panel filled with these cells can produce two kilowatts of electricity, about one-quarter of the power a typical house uses annually. The cost of a two-kilowatt system and a battery backup is about $20,000, but rebates and tax write-offs can cut the costs, as can federal and state programs and the federal requirement that utilities buy back excess power.

Solar photovoltaic panels on a roof collect energy from the sun for conversion to electricity. Federal law requires utilities to buy excess from consumers.

An integral collector-storage system features one or more black tanks or tubes in an insulated, glazed box. Cold water first passes through the solar collector, which preheats the water. The water then continues on to the conventional backup water heater, providing a reliable source of hot water.

■ Fast Facts on Saving Energy

Set the air conditioner's thermostat at 78 degrees or higher, the furnace's thermostat at 68 degrees or lower (health permitting). Three percent to 5 percent more energy is used for each degree the furnace is set above 68 degrees and for each degree the air conditioner is set below 78 degrees. Clean or replace filters regularly. Set the water heater thermostat at 140 degrees or "normal." If you have a dishwasher, check to see if you can use 120-degree water (a "low" setting on the water heater). Do only full dishwasher loads and use the shortest cycle that will get your dishes clean. If operating instructions allow, turn off the dishwasher before the drying cycle, open the door, and let the dishes air-dry.

Fix dripping faucets. A single hot water faucet can waste 212 gallons a month, which not only increases water bills, but also increases the bill for heating the water. Defrost refrigerators and freezers before ice buildup becomes one-quarter-inch thick.Put a lid on pots to reduce cooking time. Match pot size to burner size. Install shades, awnings, or sunscreens on windows facing south and west to block summer light. In winter, open shades on sunny days to help warm rooms. Wrap your hot water tank in an insulating "blanket" if it feels warm to the touch. Use warm or cold water for laundry, rinse in cold, and wash when you have full loads.

Follow a professional home energy audit at www.remodelingonthemoney.com

High energy prices are making Americans get serious about reducing energy consumption. The American Institute of Architects (AIA) reports that a survey of its members found that to address rapidly escalating home energy costs, homeowners are reacting with a sharp increase in preference for energy-efficient management systems and products.

According to the AIA: "Our data indicate that consumers are becoming increasingly aware of the energy-efficient options that are available in the marketplace, and they are requesting that architects incorporate them into the design and remodeling of their homes."

■ ASSESS YOUR ENERGY USE

If you are concerned that your house isn't as tight as it could be, you could start with a home energy audit. A professional audit costs $300 to $500 for four to eight hours' work, and should include a detailed, room-by-room analysis, including a blower-door test and a thermographic scan.

A blower door is a fan mounted into an exterior door frame. The fan pulls air out of the house, lowering the air pressure inside. The higher outside air pressure then flows in through all unsealed cracks and openings. Thermography, or infrared scanning, measures surface temperatures—the light in the heat spectrum—with video and still cameras that record the temperature variations of the building's skin. The tests are designed to check for air leaks and to determine where insulation should be installed, or whether the insulation already there has been put in improperly.

If you perform the audit yourself, make a list of what you find in your walk-through and then decide the order in which you will tackle your problems. Check for air leaks around

Though washers, dishwashers, refrigerators, and room air conditioners have ENERGY STAR labels, clothes dryers do not. That is because they all use about the same amount of energy and comply with minimum standards established by the U.S. Department of Environmental Protection.

High-efficiency condensing furnaces come in both oil and gas models, and typically have efficiency ratings of 90 percent or more. They recycle the heat, and the gas furnaces have no pilot light so there is no waste there, and they are vented directly to the outside, usually through PVC pipes through the basement wall so heat generated stays in the house and isn't wasted up the chimney.

Too often, people add electric baseboard heat to supplement poorly operating heating systems. The solution is not to increase the sources of heat, but to tighten up the house enough so you can downsize the heating source.

Evacuated-tube solar collectors feature parallel rows of transparent glass tubes. Each tube contains a glass outer tube and metal absorber tube attached to a fin. The fin's coating absorbs solar energy but inhibits radiative heat loss.

windows and doors, pipes, and electrical outlets. If your house is not insulated, see whether insulation would help cut the heat loss. If it has insulation, it might not be enough to meet federal recommendations. For example, if you have less than 11 to 12 inches of attic insulation, you probably need more.

If you have forced-air heat, change the filters regularly for more efficient operation, not just once in the fall and once in the spring.

Some people take energy efficiency seriously and won't leave achieving it to anyone else. Yet while aiming for energy efficiency, Stephen has tried to keep as much of the character as possible of the house he has been renovating for 20 years, recycling much of the original material.

Oddly enough, it is an all-electric house with a high-efficiency heat pump. The pump and all the heavy-duty users of electricity are on an off-peak meter, which means the power used is half price per kilowatt-hour. Every year, the 2,800-square-foot house uses 11,520 kilowatt-hours of electricity, costing $1,200. There are people who might ask how he can put heat on an off-peak meter without risking a cold house, but he's confident that it isn't going to happen.

A 50-gallon capacity conventional hot water gas heater in a basement. Most of the energy consumed by these heaters is to keep standing water warm.

Air leakage amounts to about 25 percent of the energy loss in a house.

■ Fast Facts on Efficient Light Bulbs

Light bulbs are synonymous with bright ideas—in cartoons, at any rate. But compact fluorescent bulbs can also be a small, yet brilliant, step toward energy efficiency. The Department of Energy says they use two-thirds less energy than incandescent bulbs and last 10 times longer.

Compact fluorescent lightbulbs (also known as CFLs) are available in different sizes and shapes, including mini spiral, spiral, and A-line, that fit almost any fixture. CFLs save electricity costs over their lifetime and prevent greenhouse gas emissions. CFLs and fixtures that use them that have earned the Environmental Protection Agency's ENERGY STAR rating produce about 70 percent less heat, so they're safer to use and can help cut energy costs associated with home cooling. (Consider that a halogen bulb in a torchiere lamp is 700 to 1,100 degrees Fahrenheit.)

When choosing the right bulb or fixture, look for one that offers the same lumen rating as the light you're replacing. Manufacturers often label these products in terms of watt replacement, which can also guide your decision making. Energy-efficient lighting will provide the same or more light while using fewer watts. Dimmers enable you to set the mood with a range of light output, but check the bulb or fixture's packaging first to be sure it will perform well on a dimmer.

For the biggest energy savings, replace incandescents or halogens with CFLs in the rooms you spend the most time in, such as your family and living rooms, kitchen, and porch. Place the bulbs in open fixtures that allow air flow.

CFLs contain very small amounts of mercury sealed within the glass tubing—an average of 5 milligrams, which is roughly equivalent to the amount of ink on the tip of a ballpoint pen. Mercury is what enables the CFL to be an efficient light source; there is currently no substitute for it, but manufacturers have been trying to reduce the amount used. CFLs are safe to use in the home. According to the Department of Energy, no mercury is released when the bulbs are in use, and they pose no danger if used properly, though care should be taken when handling because the tubing is glass.

If no other disposal options are available except the trash can, place CFLs in a sealed plastic bag. Never send a CFL or other mercury-containing product to an incinerator.

GreenGuard® RainDrop® housewrap, the industry's first woven housewrap with water drainage channels that move bulk water down to the base of the exterior wall (Photo courtesy of Pactiv Inc.).

Stephen's house is heavily insulated everywhere that wouldn't detract from the appearance with R-30 to R-35 urethane spray-on foam and extruded polystyrene in the attic, R-19 to R-22 insulation in the walls, and R-11 in the basement. In addition, there's a high-efficiency wood-burning stove in the living room that can be put to use when necessary, and which he used as the chief source of heat for 15 years, until his two children came along and he was worried about them being cold. They had also spent a great deal of time chopping wood and hauling it into the house.

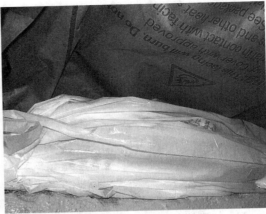

Air leaks can be sealed with a piece of unfaced insulation in a plastic kitchen bag. Any gaps around the seal can be filled with foam insulation.

The carpeting in Stephen's house is recycled. The paints are water-based. The family uses adjustable low-flow showerheads and low-flow toilets; standard faucets release water at more than twice the rate of low-flows and old toilets use 3.5 gallons to flush. All their appliances are ENERGY STAR–rated.

The house has a solar water heater with recycled collectors and an 80-gallon solar tank with a photovoltaic-activated pump. The radiant heat system below the kitchen floor was an experiment, and because of the way Stephen installed it, did not warm the entire floor consistently. Still, 99 percent isn't bad, and he eventually plans to try solar radiant floor heating.

Pellet stoves are an alternative to wood for homeowners. The stoves burn pellets made of compressed sawdust and corn, among other clean sources of fuel, are highly energy efficient, and vent to the outside.

For every degree of thermostat setback over a 24-hour period, a homeowner should reduce heat consumption by 3 percent. Experts suggest that homeowners set the temperature at 68 degrees during the day when they're home and then to set it back to 55 at night or when they are at work. A well-insulated, tight house shouldn't fall to 55 degrees overnight.

■ INSULATING YOUR HOME

Kent, who has built 125 affordable houses for low- and middle-income buyers for over

30 years, has developed a taste for the energy efficient and environmentally friendly, both of which are made manifest in House No. 126. At the top of his list of efficient materials are the wall panels that come in sizes up to 40 feet long, are made of polystyrene, and are reinforced with galvanized 18-gauge steel tubes. They are fire-proof and termite resistant.

"We were looking for high-tech components that required low-tech, on-site construction that could be done with a crew of seven," Kent said. "Instead of having to rent a crane for $500 a day, we used a simple block-and-tackle arrangement over a steel beam to hoist the second-floor panels into place." Kent used the panels for an addition on one of the two rehab projects he's working on. The system allowed him to get two more bed-rooms on the third floor of the new house, for a total of five bedrooms and two-and-a-half baths.

Kent also was looking to keep waste at a minimum. Little wood is used in the construction—just some plywood for the sub-floors, pressure-treated lumber for the sills, and a Glulam (engineered wood) beam that supports the roof. To attach drywall to the interior walls and fiber-cement siding to the exterior ones, his crew routed channels for two-by-three-inch steel studs in the panels and used them to frame the window openings as well. The panels required no poured footings, just a four-inch floor.

Kent prefers fiber-cement siding to vinyl because fiber cement is recycled and recyclable and lasts 50 years. He was so convinced of its quality that he actually removed vinyl from nearby houses he had rehabbed and replaced it with fiber-cement siding. Kent also decided to install a standing-seam metal roof that will accommodate 18-foot-long solar panels in two

Johns Manville produces a formaldehyde-free insulation. The resin used in the manufacture of the product feels softer and isn't as itchy as standard fiberglass. The content is certified 25 percent recycled and can be recycled after use. It increases air quality and cuts drafts and noise.

Have ducts tested for air leakage, which can reduce the efficiency of your heating system by up to 30 percent. Seal leaks with mastic or non-cloth-backed tape labeled UL181 B-FX.

Open chimney flues in nonworking fireplaces and dirty radiator coils that help return hot water rather than cold to the boiler are among the worst contributors to heat loss.

The Alliance to Save Energy recom-mends a 7-degree setback, but only when you are out of the house or in bed at night (high setting 72 degrees, low 65). The important point is that the Alliance recommends using program-mable thermostats so you can save energy when the house is empty, but not setting heat to an uncomfortable level when you are in the house.

■ Fast Facts on Insulation

Tightening up your house against the cold can mean any number of things, but one of the best and often least expensive ways is sealing air leaks and insulating. This prompts the question: What kind of insulation should you use? That depends on your house and all sorts of other factors, such as the following:

First things first: Talk about insulation means talk about R-values. Insulation material has pockets of trapped air that prevent heat from penetrating it. R-value measures how well the material resists that heat transfer. The higher the R-value, the better the resistance.

Some types of insulation are relatively simple for a do-it-yourselfer to handle. Insulating blankets come as batts (precut pieces) or in rolls, and may have a paper or aluminum-foil facing that acts as a vapor retardant. Blankets are made of fiberglass (spun from molten sand and glass); rock wool, a man-made concoction of natural minerals; or slag wool, made from iron-ore blast-furnace slag, an industrial waste product. These types can be used in unfinished walls, floors, and ceilings where the spacing is standard (studs or joists 16 inches or 25 inches on center), and where there are no obstructions such as water pipes, electrical wiring, or gas lines.

Reflective insulation includes foil-faced paper, polyethylene bubbles, and plastic film. It, too, fits well between studs and joists in unfinished spaces, with the foil-faced polyethylene bubbles most suitable for cavities with obstructions.

Be sure to ask if some other kind of insulation, such as those best installed by professionals, would be better for your home. For example, there is blown-in insulation, which is usually cellulose, a product made of ground-up newspapers treated with boron. Be sure you don't overinsulate with this, however, because the weight of cellulose and the fact that it settles over time means it can cause drywall ceilings to sag.

Increasingly popular is foam insulation. It's typically made of polyurethane, has high R-values, doesn't shrink or settle once in place, blocks drafts caused by air infiltration because it conforms to every nook and cranny, and offers a barrier to moisture. Rigid foam insulation, commonly made from fiberglass, polystyrene, or polyurethane, comes in a variety of thicknesses with insulating values of R-4 to R-8 per inch. Indoors, it has to be covered with half-inch gypsum board or other building code–approved material for fire safety.

According to an extensive Internet search, R-19 fiberglass batts are running about 41 cents a square foot; R-38 batts, 86 cents. Cellulose insulation is running 8 cents a square foot uninstalled.

Adding insulation to an attic is relatively easy and cost-effective. To find out if you have enough, the U.S. Department of Energy suggests measuring the thickness of the insulation. If it is less than R-22 (seven inches of fiberglass or rock wool or six inches of cellulose), you could probably benefit by adding more. Most U.S. homes should have between R-22 and R-49 insulation in the attic.

For rooms that are uncomfortable, this booster fan fits over the room vent and begins operating once the built-in thermostat reaches a set temperature.

sections of eight panels each. Metal roofs contain about 60 percent recycled material and absorb 34 percent less heat than asphalt shingles.

The wall panels Kent used have high insulation values, with R-50 for a 12-inch roof panel and R-30 for the walls. The house is so tight that, in combination with active and passive solar innovations, it was tough finding a heating system small enough for the house. The solution was close to what Kent wanted: a Canadian-made clean air furnace that uses a 40,000-BTU domestic water heater as its heat source and has a built-in heat-recovery system that replaces stale air with fresh.

In that ever-changing air inside the house, Kent is also going green with renewable bamboo flooring in the common areas and cork flooring in the bedrooms—both of which are discussed in chapter 15.

A booster fan ($40) fits on the nearest heating vent and plugs into a nearby outlet. It can be programmed to start boosting heat flow when the furnace comes on.

■ KEEPING COOL

There are several ways to cool your home, including window air conditioners and central air-conditioning, as well as energy-efficient techniques for keeping in cold air.

Green tip: Look for wall coverings made of paper or natural fiber rather than synthetic materials, and printed with natural inks.

■ Fast Facts on Insulating Crawlspaces

How one insulates a crawlspace depends on whether the space is ventilated or unventilated.

Traditionally, crawlspaces have been vented to prevent problems with moisture; many building codes require vents. Construction professionals now recognize that building an unventilated crawlspace (or closing vents after the crawlspace dries out after construction) is the best option in homes using proper moisture control and exterior drainage techniques.

Here's what to do:

Eliminate or seal the foundation vents. Ensure that combustion furnaces and water heaters located in the crawlspace are sealed-combustion units equipped with a powered combustion system. Seal all air leaks through the exterior wall during and after construction, including the band joist.

Locate the crawlspace access inside the home or install an access through the perimeter that will remain airtight after repeated use. Install rigid foam board or batt insulation—exterior foam, interior foam, or interior batt—to achieve complete insulation coverage. Insulate the band joist with batt insulation as well as the crawlspace access if it's located in the wall.

Install a continuous termite shield between the band joist and masonry foundation wall that covers the wall insulation and extends completely outside (or leave a two- to four-inch insulation gap at the top for termite inspection). Install a supply outlet in the crawlspace, relying on the leakiness of the floor to provide the return air path.

Choosing a central air-conditioning system must be done carefully. The best ones are efficient, operating on minimal electricity to hold utility bills down. They provide steady, dependable performance year after year when properly maintained. Good systems are quiet, long lasting, and low in service needs.

Obviously, an air conditioner that's too small won't keep your home sufficiently cool, but what many don't realize is that an oversized system will cycle (turn on and off) more than necessary, wasting expensive energy and possibly putting undue strain on the compressor. An air-conditioning dealer's job

Tyvek is a house wrap building membrane, used to limit air leakage, and still allow breathability.

is to determine the optimum size for your home by making a careful study of your cooling requirements. These include window dimensions and exposure, floor space, insulation and local climate, heat-generating appliances, the direction your home faces, and even the amount of your home's exterior shaded by trees.

The dealer also will specify the cooling capacity of the system in either BTUs of heat that will be removed each hour, or refrigeration tons, with one ton being equal to 12,000 BTUs per hour. Air conditioner manufacturers are required by law to evaluate and rate their equipment according to its energy efficiency. This rating is known in the industry as a SEER, or Seasonal

> As fuel costs increase, the payback period for improving your home's insulation is growing shorter, to two years from five.

> A full-blown green home can cost 3 percent to 5 percent more than a conventional house, but lenders and Fannie Mae are offering incentives through energy-efficient mortgages to make such houses more attractive.

■ Fast Facts on Doing Your Own Insulation Work

Gather the tools required, which are minimal: staple gun for installation; utility knife, tape measure, and straight edge for measuring and cutting. Wear a long-sleeve shirt with collar and cuffs buttoned, gloves, a hat, safety goggles, and a disposable dust respirator.

Don't cover or pack insulation around bare stove pipes, electrical fixtures, or recessed lighting fixtures. Building and fire codes prohibit installation of thermal insulation within three inches of a recessed fixture enclosure or above the fixture so that it will trap heat and prevent free circulation of air, unless the fixture is identified by label as suitable for insulation to be in direct contact with the fixture.

If you have an old house, you should first have the wiring checked by an electrician to see whether it is safe. Most older attics have the original knob-and-tube wiring that might not be in good shape.

Don't cover attic vents. Proper ventilation, especially in attics, must be maintained to avoid overheating in summer and moisture buildup all year long.

When installing batts and rolls on unfinished attic floors, work from the perimeter toward the attic door. If you are putting in more insulation, use unfaced batts and put them perpendicular to the old ones because that will help to cover the tops of the joists themselves and reduce heat loss or gain through the frame.

Be sure to insulate the attic access door. Not doing so can cancel out much of the energy savings achieved through insulating the attic.

■ Fast Facts on Window Air Conditioners

Apartment dwellers and homeowners who can afford to install central air-conditioning need to know the right size and the most efficient energy level before they buy.

Be sure to consider the size of the room you want to cool, how big the windows are, and the ceiling height. You should also consider whether the space is insulated and whether it is fully exposed to the sun in the afternoon, which is the hottest time of the day. All these issues factor into the air conditioner capacity you'll need. Most capacity is rated in British thermal units (BTUs) per hour. The people at Fedders, the air conditioner manufacturer, recommend a 7,000-BTU unit for a 250-square-foot room; add 4,000 BTUs if the room is a kitchen to compensate for the heat from ovens and dishwashers. Brick houses and rooms with high ceilings also require larger-capacity units.

Don't make the common mistake of buying an oversize unit—it won't cool the space better. In fact, it will cost more to operate and will be less effective on hot, humid days because it will remove heat quickly but will remove only some of the humidity. The result will be a cool but clammy room.

Be sure to ask whether the unit has motorized louvers, which distribute cool air flow more evenly; some units have louvers that must be adjusted manually. Also ask whether the unit can be switched from outside air to recirculating. Set the dial to outside air when you want to refresh the air in the room. Switch to recirculate on the hottest days so the air conditioner's job—keeping cool air cool—is easier.

You cannot safely plug an air conditioner into an extension cord, so make sure there is an appropriate outlet nearby. Units that draw less than 7.5 amps of electricity can be plugged directly into any 15- or 20-amp household circuit not shared with another major appliance. A larger air conditioner requires its own 230-volt circuit.

The unit you buy won't necessarily fit into any window, unless your house is new or you've replaced your windows recently. If you own an older house, you might need to use cardboard or rolled-up plastic to fill in gaps and get the unit to fit properly. If the air conditioner isn't fitted tightly in the window, it will be noisier, cause the window to vibrate, and allow cool air to escape. This means it will take longer and cost more to make the room comfortable.

Don't forget that an air conditioner can be heavy, up to 90 pounds. Get help lifting it into and out of the window.

The typical window air conditioner costs between $250 and $800. The more energy efficient the unit, the more it tends to cost.

Every new air conditioner displays an energy efficiency rating (EER), a number between 8 and 13. The higher the EER, the more efficient the model and the lower your electrical use.

The right amount of insulation and ventilation can keep you warm and comfortable during all kinds of weather. Find what you need to know at www.remodelingonthemoney.com

Energy Efficiency Rating, and the higher the SEER, the more efficient the equipment. Most new homes with central air come equipped with a standard builder's model. However, when replacement becomes necessary, property owners can upgrade their air-conditioning by specifying a more energy-efficient system. High SEER models are generally more expensive, but can easily make up the difference by reducing your home energy bills over the long run.

The compressor is the heart of a condensing unit. On a hot day, it works long and hard, and you should find one that does so quietly. Look for condensers that have louvered steel cabinets that protect the coils from damage and expensive repair bills. Many municipalities require that compressors be shielded from the street by trees or fences that are designed to reduce noise. Check the local building code.

The key to a central air-conditioning purchase is the dealer and the manufacturer. You should try to buy from someone local who works with a well-known manufacturer producing a recognized brand name. Warranties are critical and service agreements are as well. You want the repair person to arrive on time and you want to make sure that he or she carries a huge supply of repair parts so you won't be left for days in the heat waiting for the gizmo to arrive.

■ STAYING WARM

The experts recommend that if you are going to change your central air-conditioning unit, you should also change your furnace. When you do both, what you are trying to create is a system that maximizes indoor comfort at minimal cost. The furnaces you should be looking at are ones

Leave plenty of time to locate "green" building products because many of them are made and installed by small companies.

Use passive solar heating on sunny days; open the drapes on south-facing windows to let the sun shine in. At night, close the drapes to retain indoor heat. Keep drapes closed over large expanses of window that don't receive direct sunlight.

"Passive cooling" means creating ways that will actually "shed" heat before it reaches the house. One way is to coat flat roofs with a white elastomeric substance that reflects the heat and keeps the interior cool. An elastomeric coating is one with rubberlike properties that will return to its original dimensions after being stretched or deformed. The coating will expand and contract with the surface to which it is applied.

According to estimates from the Energy Information Administration, in just two decades U.S. energy consumption will increase by almost 40 percent—an amount equivalent to the energy used today in California, Texas, New York, Ohio, Pennsylvania, and Illinois.

If your furnace does not have a built-in humidifier, use a portable unit in frequently occupied areas such as the bedroom and living room. The additional moisture will increase the heat index inside your home, making 68 degrees feel more like 76.

that are efficient, dependable, quiet, long-lasting, and require little expensive service.

When a furnace loses or wastes heat, it requires more energy to keep your home warm. Some furnaces lose heat through the walls of the furnace cabinet. Energy-efficient furnaces significantly reduce this loss with a blanket of insulation that lines the inside of the cabinet walls. When a gas furnace is not in operation, most send a steady, wasteful draft of warm household air traveling up the venting system and out the roof. Some, however, have an induced draft blower that works in conjunction with a hot surface ignition system to pull hot gases through the heat exchanger at a constant and controlled rate of flow. As the burner cycles off, the draft blower stops, keeping the heating air in the system.

Pilot lights also can be wasteful. An electric ignition eliminates the need for a constantly burning pilot. This feature alone can result in an efficiency level that is 6 percent higher than other furnaces, and combined with an induced draft blower, the efficiency rating can be improved by 20 percent or more.

Most gas furnaces vent combustion by-products and gases by allowing the warm air to rise naturally. However, on occasion, proper venting of combustion by-products may be restricted due to blockage, deterioration of venting systems, malfunctions, or other causes. An induced draft blower maintains a constant draft through the heat exchanger, which ensures proper venting of the furnace combustion chamber. Some furnaces also feature a pressure switch that continuously monitors venting; and in the event it senses a vent flow restriction, it will automatically shut down your heating system for your safety.

The most efficient furnaces tap the energy of the hot vent gases, which can reach temperatures of 500 degrees Fahrenheit and more. Some furnaces route hot gases through a secondary heat exchanger that will capture wasted heat and use it instead to preheat household air for efficiency ratings in excess of 92 percent. A high-efficiency furnace generally wears a higher price tag, but it can make up the difference by reducing operating costs over the long run.

Some furnaces are better than others, and you should look for one that includes heat exchangers that resist corrosion, direct-drive blower units, induced draft blowers, pressure switches, and an insulated blower compartment, which helps minimize operating noise. You also should ask your dealer if the manufacturer of the brand you're considering quality-checks and tests

---

■ **Fast Facts on Sealing Air Leaks**

Insulate areas near exterior penetrations such as electrical service, plumbing lines, telephone/TV cables, ductwork for vents and fans, and the flue pipe into the chimney. Insulate areas near penetrations to your attic or basement, electrical wiring, and fixtures, and plumbing supply and waste lines.

Caulk the sill plate around the perimeter of the house from the exterior, if it is accessible.

Weather-strip/insulate your attic access panel. Install gaskets beneath receptacle and switch cover plates.

If you are replacing the siding on your house, take that opportunity to install exterior air barrier or house wrap.

---

every unit before it leaves the plant. Be sure to check out the terms of the warranty. Service, too, is a critical factor in buying a new heating system.

Andrew believes that today's complicated lives have unnecessarily added to energy needs. He has found, for example, that the refrigerator consumes the most power in a typical house, hands down. Second at his house was the fish tank, so he solved the problem by removing the heater. (The fish began laying eggs because they turned out to be cold-water fish.)

With a wood fire and a shot of heat from the gas furnace in the morning and again just before his wife, Joyce, arrives home from work, Andrew can keep their house, which was built in 1917, at 68 degrees in the winter. Cooling comes from a third-floor room air conditioner used only six times in a typical summer.

In 1998, the local utility changed its rate structure to allow homeowners to generate their own electric power and sell it back to the utility through an energy cooperative, which means that the couple's 2.7-kilowatt solar photovoltaic system on the back roof, after generating what the couple needs to live, uploads surplus power to the utility grid, causing the electric meter to spin backward.

■ OTHER ENERGY-SAVING TIPS

Other energy-saving measures include flow restrictors on the faucets, water-saving showerheads, a high-efficiency gas boiler and refrigerator, fluorescent lighting, and skylights. Water from the roof drains into the organic garden.

Kitchen waste and leaves are collected for compost. On sunny days, household water is preheated by two drain-down solar hot water panels mounted on the sunroom roof. If the sun does not heat the water enough, a direct-vent water heater takes over.

Everything is metered to determine energy use. In 2001, Andrew and Joyce generated 491 more kilowatt-hours of electricity than they used, so they paid just a $61 customer service fee to the utility. In 2002, they paid just that same $61 customer service fee. In 1993, their electric bill was $570 a year. The entire system cost $26,000.

Energy-efficiency and green or sustainable building requires a whole-house approach, but sometimes what the experts and manufacturers advise may not work in your house. "Generalizations can't be applied to every home," Andrew says. "Homes not only have unique designers and builders when they are built, but they have been remodeled and renovated over the years. In addition, the attitudes and behaviors and number of people living in them vary with each home."

The bottom line: It's all about comfort.

Not Older, but Better

>"I've been independent all my life, and I won't stop now."

—Lena ColOgrossi, age 92

There's absolutely no reason why Lena shouldn't be able to live by herself. Except for a couple of bad knees that have slowed her a bit in the past few years, she continues to live in the suburban rancher that she and her late husband, Adam, bought in the early 1970s after the last of their children left their three-story Victorian house in a nearby city.

When Adam became sick in 1990, she was able to care for him with the aid of a visiting nurse and her children, until he died just short of his 90th birthday. Even today, she continues to drive a car around her community, visiting her children, grandchildren, and great-grandchildren; grocery shopping; and singing with the senior citizens' center choir that travels to area nursing homes "to entertain the old people," as Lena says.

Everything in Lena's house is on that first floor, and two accessible bathrooms flank the master bedroom. The washer and dryer, both front-loading so she could reach them if she were confined to a wheelchair, are between the kitchen and the back porch—actually a deck/porch with ceiling fan where she sits in the summer. The kitchen where she produces her tangy pasta sauce (the secret is a cherry pepper) is designed so she can easily work and cook without having to stretch or bend.

> A two-story elevator these days only adds $15,000 to $17,000 to the price of a new home, while 10 years ago it was $25,000 to $40,000.

Lena has had some loss of sight in one of her eyes over the years, and is concerned that the problem could spread to the other one. It worries her that she might have to stop driving, which would cause her to change her lifestyle, but she asserts that she'll never let it get her down, and that she will remain independent and in her house for years to come.

Consider that Lena remains on her own a couple more years into her 90th decade, and then look at older houses and how virtually unaccommodating they would be to even someone as active and resourceful as she. In cities and in near suburbs in older parts of the United States,

Levers rather than knobs are easier for people with arthritis to use. In addition, this lever is at wheelchair-user level.

> Almost 20 percent of the population has some level of disability, and 10 percent describe the disability as severe. The vast majority of those are adults 45 or older, the same group that will be the chief consumers of move-up housing for at least the next 20 years.

where vast quantities of the housing stock predates World War II, elderly and disabled people struggle up flights of stairs, strain to reach for light switches, and have trouble getting wheelchairs through rooms and out of the front door to make it to medical appointments or simply to visit friends and neighbors.

When Lena was born in 1914, the lifespan of the typical American was 45, and the people who did reach her age were healthy and active enough to not let a flight of stairs get in their way. No thought was given to designing a house that someone could continue to occupy in various life stages from birth to death. In those days, electricity, telephones, and indoor plumbing were new, and builders were having enough trouble working those revolutionary inventions in houses.

That was then. The concept of retirement is only about 50 years old for the vast majority of Americans; yet it is something on which the baby-boomer generation appears to be focused as an estimated 78 million of those born between 1947 and 1964 begin to enter what some refer

GFCI outlets should be installed in normally damp spaces such as kitchens, bathrooms, basements and out of doors. Switches for lights and heater fans in the ceiling are accessible from a wheelchair.

to as "active-adult status"—not quite ready to retire but eager to begin planning for it.

While statistics show that the demand for accessible housing is growing, many builders remain concerned about the costs of changes

> Bathrooms in all houses should be built with reinforced walls for installation of grab bars in the future.

needed to make houses and apartments barrier-free, and how such changes—first-floor master suites and ramps, for example—will affect resale values.

A study commissioned by the U.S. Department of Housing and Urban Development (HUD) has found that if builders comply with the *Fair Housing Act* during construction, their dwelling-unit costs increase by one-half of 1 percent. Remodeling a building can cost a great deal more.

Many boomers and others will head to warmer climates or to communities for older adults. The vast majority, however, will prefer to find some way of accommodating their present home—close to family and familiar things—to the changing needs that age will bring. The concept is called "aging in place," and the instrument of accommodation is known as "universal

A stacked front-loading washer and dryer are easily accessible for those in wheelchairs. Keeping them on the first floor or adjacent to living areas makes them even more accessible.

■ Fast Facts on Aging in Place

Install handrails on both sides of all steps (inside and outside).

Secure all carpets and area rugs with double-sided tape.

Install easy-to-grasp handles for all drawers and cabinet doors.

Use brighter lightbulbs in all settings.

Install nightlights in all areas of night activity.

Add reflective, nonslip tape on all non-carpeted stairs.

Install lever handles for all doors.

Place a bench near entrances for setting down purchases and resting.

Install closet lights as well as adjustable rods and shelves.

Install rocker light switches; consider illuminated ones in select areas.

Eighteen months after its vice president first read about the effects of arthritis on the baby-boomer generation, Fiskars developed a prototype called the "Golden Age Scissors," based on consideration for users with arthritis. The lightweight design accommodates both right- and left-handers equally well and offers a larger, softer grip to distribute pressure more evenly across the palm of the hand. The scissors also incorporates a lock closure and a spring assist for opening.

Duracell came up with the EasyTab for installing its tiny hearing aid batteries, which were introduced to help make hearing aids digital and less detectable.

In the 1980s, the second-floor master was designed as a getaway from growing children and their heavy metal music and noisy friends. Today, having a master suite on the first floor means fewer trips upstairs for aging boomers.

Although they aren't marketed as such, the Grips line of utensils from Oxo are perfect for people who are having problems from arthritis.

design." Universal, or flexible, design employs features that allow a house to grow with changes in needs and lifestyles.

While many new home builders have not been eager to embrace universal design for a variety of reasons, the Remodelers Council of the National Association of Home Builders takes it seriously enough to have created certification for remodelers through courses that result in designations for specialized skills, such as dealing with the growing number of people who want their houses modified so they can stay there as they age. The certification was designed to counter suspicions that older consumers have about remodeling contractors.

One obvious example of universal design is placing the master suite on the first floor of a house. If the design is flexible, the master suite can effectively become a self-contained apartment for a spouse or relative who must use a wheelchair. Having a door that opens from the bedroom onto a patio within easy reach of a car in the driveway allows the disabled occupant unencumbered access.

The universal design philosophy takes two trends into account. One is that people 45 and older buying trade-up housing do not plan to move frequently. The other is that as people age, they progressively will have trouble doing everyday tasks, such as reaching down to open a kitchen drawer, reaching up to get a book on the top shelf of the bookcase, or stepping over the raised base of a shower stall without having something to grab on to.

Universal design features make the house accessible to everyone, not just those having increasing problems with accessibility. This includes front-loading washers and dryers,

Scuffed from use, but this threshold from dining room to kitchen is designed for barrier-free access. The quarry tile kitchen floor is virtually slip-proof. The door clearance is 30 inches.

Grab bars are easily installed during renovation. They need to be secured to the studs behind the tile.

ovens with side hinges, and electrical outlets you can use without getting down on your hands and knees. It also includes lever-handle doors and faucet hardware throughout the house; recessed door fronts on base cabinets for wheelchair access to sinks; a staircase that can easily be retrofitted for a chair lift; and a no-threshold shower in the master bath.

Some houses include flexible "bonus" space that can accommodate a live-in nurse if that becomes necessary.

"Barrier free" is another term that can be applied to universal design. Until his mother-in-law's stroke three years ago resulted in her using a wheelchair, John acknowledges he hadn't given much thought to how people deal with disabilities day to day. What he realized is that the need for accessible housing is only going to increase as the population ages. As John got deeper into research on the topic, he also discovered that accessibility issues are not limited to older people, but include young men and women who must use wheelchairs because of illness or accidents.

The house John built provides access to the front door by a ramp with a gradual slope rather than steps. All the doors except those for the pantry and one of the closets are 36 inches wide, which means that someone in a wheelchair can easily get through.

All doors have levers rather than knobs. The windows are casement and open and close by turning a crank. Each window has a lever lock at the bottom. In the kitchen, there are kneeholes under the sink and the cooktop so that a person in a wheelchair can get close enough to work. The oven is built into the cabinets rather than stand alone, with controls on the front that look like the keypad on

Forty percent of women over 50 have arthritis.

Learn about universal design at www.remodelingonthemoney.com

■ Fast Facts on Kitchen Accommodations

Modifications to kitchens to make them accommodating to older people include the following:

Raised dishwasher

Contrast colors with cabinet and wall; contrasting border in flooring around cabinets and countertop to help with low vision

Task lighting

Roll-under sink; recessed, covered plumbing; levered faucet

Variable-height counters; stove with controls on the front

Side-by-side refrigerator with counter next to it for food placement/preparation

Microwave that is accessible from seated position

Adequate turn space for wheelchair

Lowered top cabinets; lazy Susan in corner cabinet; loop pulls on cabinets

a microwave. The floors are tile or hardwood, with no carpeting that might make rolling across on a wheelchair difficult. The closets can be customized so that the height of the shelves can meet the homeowner's needs.

There is a large bathroom with a shower stall that has a fold-down seat. The shower has a slight lip, no more than an inch, and John plans on doing something to make for an easier access. The way it is now, however, allows the person in the wheelchair to slide off the chair and into the shower seat easily.

Another threshold, this one from the dining room to the bathroom, is designed to permit wheelchair and walker users easy access from one room to another. The older basket-weave tile is not slip-proof, however. The door clearance is 30 inches.

One positive development has been the recent proliferation of companies that produce household items designed to make life easier for the disabled. These include electronic-sensor faucets, built-in seats in showers, and motorized scooters.

When she was finally unable to live on her own, Dorothy moved to another city to be with her son, William, an architect. He wanted her to be able to live safely on her own but surrounded by familiar things. Dorothy, a former teacher, had lost sight in one eye completely several years before, and was facing the same problem in her other eye. William owned a two-story commercial building—a former veal processing plant—and decided to make accommodations that were not perfectly acceptable under the standards of the *Americans with Disabilities Act*, but would meet the everyday requirements of many people with disabilities.

William's chief goal was to condense his mother's world while preserving it—keeping what was absolutely necessary to soften the

Nine-foot windows are being added to housing to allow additional light that people will find necessary as they age, but no one comes right out and says that's the reason for them.

Ramp construction should follow the rules. It should be designed to minimize puddling from rainstorms and with a nonslip surface, as well as having well-placed landings to allow the wheelchair-bound person a safe place to pause to rest.

An accessible elevator that can be installed in an existing house as a retrofit, as well as in new construction. The cost of installation in either case is falling each year.

■ Fast Facts on Exterior Accommodations

Exterior renovations can include the following:

Extra-wide, single-car garage; ramped entrance from garage

Zero-level entry to main entrance using graded sidewalk; brush-concrete sidewalk provides traction

Handrails

Security system, including video cameras; intercom system throughout the home

Wide front porch with easy wheelchair access

Doorway with glass panels to see approaching visitors

One of the earliest entries into universal design was Cuisinart with its food processor that had controls and attachments that were easy to use and install. There is even a Cuisinart tea kettle

■ Fast Facts on Ramp Design

A ramp should have a gentle slope. The higher your ramp is, the longer it needs to be. There should be at least 12 inches of ramp for every 1 inch that the ramp has to climb.

Ramps look better if they are close to the house. A ramp that is 30 feet long will be easier to use if it has a flat landing in the middle where the user can take a rest.

There should be a landing every time the ramp changes direction.

The ramp and landings must be level from side to side. If a ramp slopes, someone using a walker has trouble balancing, and a wheelchair becomes hard to steer.

Make sure rainwater doesn't pool on the ramp surface or fall directly on the ramp from the roof. Make sure the surface of the ramp won't be slippery when wet—installing grip tape strips along the ramp and landings will help.

Install wood handrails 18 inches from the surface on both sides of the ramp.

effects of the move, while reducing the contents of a two-story house. That was complicated by the fact that his mother's favorite furnishings had been made by his father, including a corner hutch that had been crafted from lumber salvaged near an abandoned mansion close to their home.

William ruled out putting his mother's apartment on the ground floor of the building

Levered faucets on the sink are designed for ease of use for those of any age.

■ Fast Facts on Interior Design

Here are some ideas on how to accommodate the interior to changing needs:

Nonglare, nonslip tile floor; low-pile Berber carpet

Contrasting colors between walls and facings/baseboard

Low-height paddle light switches; raised electrical outlets

Easy-care, easy-to-operate windows

Thirty-six-inch-wide doors throughout first floor; open floor plan

Innovative attic truss system, which provides room for upper level to be finished as caregiver suite (bedroom, full bathroom, kitchenette, living area)

Less expensive than an elevator retrofit is a chair that can ride between floors on a rail attached to wall studs. The cost may be covered under health plans.

because his office was there. That's when the second floor—a 950-square-foot, relatively open space once rented as an artist's loft—became the solution. It would require an elevator to get there, but accommodating one was not beyond the realm of possibility because the building already had a shaft from its deboning-plant days that could be easily, though expensively, extended. The second floor also had a large, tiled bathroom with a double shower, once used by plant employees at the end of their workdays. In that space, William crafted a wheelchair-accessible shower from pieces, including a seat, bought at a home center. Removable foam on the floor of the shower leveled the space with the bathroom floor outside. He spent less than $1,000 crafting the shower, after seeing estimates of more than $3,000 for prefab models.

To help him design the new space, William photographed his mother's house so that she would have three or four views; he made an effort to replicate such things as her sitting in the den, looking out the window at the maple tree in the yard, so it would ease the transition.

Entry is easy. Near the front door is a concrete ramp with a two-tiered railing. The end at the sidewalk can be lowered even farther for easier wheelchair access. The door to the building opens out, permitting a 90-degree turn. It was designed so that a person in a wheelchair could enter easily.

■ Fast Facts on Master Suite Accommodations

Master bathroom:

Grab bars; full-size, roll-in shower with seat; adjustable-height handheld shower

Levered faucets

Telephone and intercom by toilet

Soaking tub

Low mirror behind sink; roll-under sink

Easy-to-reach storage

Master bedroom:

On first floor

Accessible closet with special built-ins

Stairways with wider treads

Recessed low-voltage lighting

Double handrails

That means anyone, not just his mother—who wasn't in a wheelchair when he began his work. In designing the entrance as he did, William answered another challenge of accessibility known as "visitability." Not only can the occupant leave and enter easily, but visitors with disabilities can as well.

It is much less expensive to adapt new houses to visitability standards. A zero-step entry for a new house costs $150, while wider interior doors cost $50. At $200, visitability amounts to about a third of the price of one bay window. To retrofit older houses, conservative estimates of the cost of a zero-step entrance is $1,000, while widening an existing doorway is as much as $700.

Once inside, you face the door of a one-stop elevator. The elevator runs from the ground to the second floor, but William figured that, rather than spend more money later on, he had to build the shaft to incorporate more floors. For safety's sake, the shaft and elevator doors have two-hour fire ratings, as well as a telephone jack for an emergency phone. To get the elevator to move, the user must close the gate, which signals a computerized mechanism that travel is safe. The final cost was about $40,000.

A hallway leads from the elevator to the door of the apartment. Clearance required to open the door and enter in a wheelchair meets or exceeds the 32-inch government standard. Because the doorstop on the bathroom could not be readjusted to a 32-inch clearance, William spent $60 on a pair of offset hinges for the bathroom door that helped him achieve that standard. In designing the apartment, William said, he examined all the standards. Again emphasizing that he was under no legal obligation to adhere to the letter of the disabilities act, he needed to see what he did need and what he couldn't do.

For example, the den in the old house of which his mother was so fond became a six-foot wall in the apartment with a TV in front of it and a chair and lamp against the opposing wall. To simulate the feeling of outdoors, William spent $20,000 adding three-foot-deep porches on the two adjacent sides of the apartment, one off the living room/den and the other in the bedroom, to the left of a sink and toilet he added so that his mother wouldn't have to find her way to the full bath during the night. The front porch, which commands a view of the river, was created by cantilevering the joists and anchoring them into the front wall. A multistory ginkgo tree is the apartment's answer to the maple at the old house.

To create plenty of sources of natural light to help his mother cope with her failing eyesight, William installed large windows and self-flashing skylights from the home center. Color is almost as important as light in accessible-housing design. For example, to help his mother find doors to rooms and the apartment itself, he painted them yellow to make them easily distinguishable from the walls.

The kitchen was a design challenge, and an expensive one at that, because all the appliances needed to be accessible from a seated position. A wall oven and separate range added up to $1,000, about three times the cost of a comparable combined version. The single sink became a double one, with the garbage disposal in the smaller side, which opened up the space under the larger sink for accessibility and storage, and because the kitchen was white, different colors of masking tape were used to distinguish cabinets, the stove and oven, and the like. A large storage closet between the kitchen and the space holding the apartment's mechanicals simulated a basement, just as the porches gave his mother access to a landscape that had the look of the yard at the old house.

In the final analysis, it was all about ingenuity. "And," William said, "ingenuity really doesn't cost that much."

A Smarter House

“Today, even wireless technology has become so inexpensive that a lot of builders are throwing it into the package, as they would a garbage disposal.”

—John Claypool, architect

7

John has been watching the progress of home automation for several years, anticipating that someday, and, as with all technological advances, fairly quickly, the smart house will become a reality for most Americans. Now, after two decades of waiting, it appears that the smart house is right around the corner.

"The vacation home that we bought a while back qualifies as a 'smart home' because you can call in a couple of numbers and turn on the heat so it is 60 degrees instead of 40 when you arrive," John said.

Bill and Marilyn have taken the smart home many steps further than John by taking their 19th-century house into the 21st century by spending almost $75,000 to "educate" it in the ways of technology. The cost, of course, is well beyond what most homeowners are willing to spend for the privilege of being able to turn on the lights in the living room and unlock the front door even before they step out of the car. Yet, in smaller ways, today's houses are getting smarter by the minute.

■ STAYING SAFE

Home security systems fall into the "everybody's doing it" category. Although the trend in new home construction since the late 1990s has been putting more focus on socialization—the front porch has become a standard part of the construction package in many areas of the country—security concerns, especially since the terrorist attacks of September 11, 2001, have reached the point where millions of homeowners, primarily in cities and near suburbs, have some sort of early warning system—either one that makes lots of noise or a sophisticated setup with links to police and fire stations.

A touchscreen allows the homeowner to control the house from a single location.

■ Fast Facts on Security Systems

If you want to install a home-security system, here are a few guidelines:

A basic security system should cost between $100 and $300. This includes a plug-in base receiver and one or more wireless magnetic sensors for doors and windows that send a signal to a receiver and automatically trigger a built-in alarm.

An expanded security system, ranging from $200 to $500, includes all elements of the basic system and a computerized device that controls lighting and appliances and has motion detectors.

A basic hardwired security system, ranging from $150 to $1,000, is a low-voltage setup that is connected to the receiver by wires. The system can be expanded to include motion sensors and smoke alarms.

An expanded hardwired system, ranging from $800 to $4,000, has all the elements of the basic system except that the receiver now controls home automation. Such systems include an automatic dialer so you can monitor what's going on at the house from the office.

■ WIRING FOR TECHNOLOGY

Home automation starts at the service center, where all outside services enter the house, including cable TV, telephone, and Internet. This central hub distributes the services to locations throughout the house in a way similar to how the electrical breaker panel controls electricity flow.

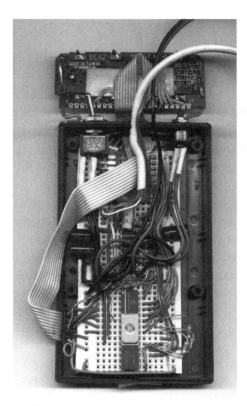

Whole-house wiring is the key to the creation of a "smart house."

You will need high-speed performance cables, specifically Category 5 or better twisted-pair cable for phone and data, and RG-6 coaxial for TV and video. Coaxial provides maximum protection from interference with your TV picture. Category 5 provides high-speed access to multiple phone lines without cross-talk. The outlets in each room determine the services available in that room and can be customized to fit the homeowners' needs.

What does this wiring allow you to do? People can work as conveniently at home as at the office. Home offices can accommodate several communications technologies so the computer, fax machine, modem, and telephone can function simultaneously while providing the efficiency of high-speed Internet access. Homes are equipped to readily accept all entertainment systems and distribution services, including direct broadcast satellite, DVD, and cable.

The homeowner has the maximum freedom and flexibility to direct audio and video services on demand to any outlet in the home—from the bedroom to home theater. The residents of the house can control heating and cooling systems more efficiently, programming them to shut down automatically to save on costs.

These systems also can be monitored for performance to anticipate problems. For instance, a worn part on the heating system will let the homeowner know when it needs to be replaced instead of having the furnace shut down in the dead of winter.

What makes Bill and Marilyn's situation unusual is that they've made an older house high-tech, and that is no easy task, unless you can afford to spend several thousand dollars

There are smart appliances that don't require a network connection, such as Whirlpool's Polara, the refrigerator/oven that debuted a few years ago, which keeps raw food at the correct temperature during the day so you can cook it right away after work.

ON-Q Home's wireless access point is connected to structured wiring, creating a secure broadband connection, allowing a wireless-device user to roam 100 meters in the home and 400 meters outside. Homeowners can add PDAs, Internet radio, and other wireless devices to their networks through the device, which looks like a smoke detector.

over and above the price of the house to do it. In new construction, wiring for home automation is easier, of course, because you just add it to the walls as you are building.

The advanced wiring necessary to make full use of technology has not, until the past five years, been near the top of the wish list of most new home buyers or builders, primarily because there continues to be a belief that the cost is prohibitive. Surveys of builders from the early 1990s found that most would be willing to install the wiring package if at least 25 percent of their buyers wanted it. At the same time, consumer surveys found that 35 percent of buyers would be willing to pay for such wiring.

Demand, of course, as well as evolving technology, has made the wiring package less expensive. In 1995, wiring costs for a 2,500-square-foot house ranged from $10,000 to $15,000, according to manufacturers. Within the next five years, the cost dropped to $5,000, and today it ranges from $750 to $1,500, those manufacturers say.

With nearly a third of Internet users on broadband, and the home networking market projected to grow from $1.8 billion in 2002 to $5.3 billion in 2007, being connected is a profit-making endeavor.

What do all these connections get you? If you hear a rustling in the yard at night, you can view the surveillance camera from the privacy of the bedroom. You can program virtually any lighting setup. You can select a music source, whether it is a CD, a music server, or the Internet, and listen to it in the kitchen, the home office, the dining area, or the bedroom. You can play different tunes in each room simultaneously.

Bill and Marilyn's house was not easy to hard wire. In an old house, all the walls are up and the plaster and lath make penetration for the Category 5 wire that carries the signals through the house

A controller for household appliances.

A smarter house doesn't need to cost a fortune. Check out the cool, yet inexpensive changes at www.remodelingonthemoney.com

slightly less than impossible. The technicians had to get the wire through the walls of four floors and two basements. It's not that the house wasn't already wired for cable and telephone, but all the wires were on the outside of the walls so the technicians simply hid them.

The idea was to restore as much of what was original about the house as possible which included the oak entry doors, without sacrificing modern conveniences. Wires for the previous alarm system had gone around the door. The wiring for the new system is inside the door and works in concert with magnetized hinges.

> Appliances that make kitchens smart are known as "hybrid white goods," a category that includes refrigerators with cable-ready TV screens or that can monitor the shelf life of the contents using bar codes; ovens that can download and execute recipes via the Internet; and ovens that can store and cook food via a cell phone.

Bill and Marilyn's security system starts with four surveillance cameras. One focuses on the front steps; another looks into the foyer. From his office on the top floor, Bill, who works from home, can see who is at the front door. If it's UPS with a delivery, he can click the delivery person in to the foyer to drop the package in front of the doors to the front hall. The other cameras, which can be viewed on each of the seven televisions in the house, are focused on vulnerable entryways. The system operates 24/7; the cameras all see in the dark and record what they see.

A video screen monitors the security system, seeing when the UPS guy is at the door.

There are motion sensors; window and door sensors; glass-break sensors; and fire, carbon monoxide, and heat sensors. The security system can be controlled with a remote device that the couple carries. When they leave the house and set the alarm, lights throughout the structure begin to shut down. When they enter the house, they click the remote, which unlocks the front door, then the inside door. Lights begin coming on and the alarm is shut off. It prevents them from having to fumble with the keys.

The iCEBOX is designed for use in the kitchen. The system allows the user access to the Internet and email. Connected to an audio/video camera, it features a home video monitor and DVD player that can play CDs. It's also a television set and has a keyboard that is washable, shockproof, and greaseproof.

In addition to security, Bill and Marilyn's system is designed to handle heating, air-conditioning, and lighting; handle music and video distribution; and act as a hub server feeding personal computers throughout the house. The system also can be integrated with other systems.

Initially, it was a desire to make the house's five-zone heating and cooling system easier to control that motivated this technologic transformation. But Bill and Marilyn soon discovered that it would be a makeover that was both costly ($40,000; $75,000 if you count several flat-screen televisions) and difficult (hard wiring required opening up the plaster walls).

Another example of integrated home automation is the addition of humidity sensors in rooms such as the bathrooms. Instead of having to turn on the exhaust fan, the system senses when the humidity in the bathroom reaches 55 percent, turns on the exhaust, which lowers the humidity to 48 percent, and shuts off automatically.

There is a central control for 80 light switches throughout the house, using software known as a UPB™ (universal powerline bus) controller. Every switch in the house has an address that can be read by the controller, and the controller can send commands to each light to do what has been programmed, such as turn on or off, dim, brighten, or set to four different scenes for both security and aesthetic lighting. There is a central wireless telephone system in almost every room, and every room has audio and video operated through a Windows Media Center, which holds 354 of the homeowners' CDs.

All wires go and come from a central control system.

Take your favorite TV shows with you everywhere. The way to do so is at www.remodelingonthemoney.com

A controller for house lamps.

■ INTERNET ACCESS

Wireless is the option many existing homeowners are turning to because the chief interest most home-owners have is warp-speed access to the Internet. Simply explained, each computer in the house either has a built-in wireless card or a port into which such a card can be plugged. One of these cards costs about $60 at an electronics store.

Say there are three computers in the house, and you want to network them to some sort of high-speed Internet access, such as a cable modem or a DSL line (both of which are explained in chapter 4 on home offices). Choose one of those computers as the central location from which the signal to all the others will be sent. Have the telephone company or the cable company install their connections at this point (first floor is best because the lines can come through the basement and up through the floor).

You'll need an Ethernet connection to a router to link all the computers to the DSL or cable modem. The Ethernet port on the router looks much like a regular phone jack, but it is slightly wider. The router, which costs about $100 but is getting less expensive, routes data

> A Slingbox is a television-streaming device that enables consumers to remotely view their cable, satellite, or digital video recorder from an Internet-enabled computer with a broadband connection. It costs around $150.

at high speeds from the connection to the rest of the network. It is typically password protected so computers in adjacent houses cannot connect or interfere with your network.

For the next few years, better Internet connections, entertainment systems, and security setups will likely be the main focus of the typical consumer—old house or new. High-tech appliances have been showpieces designed to make the

HAI's Omnistat provides simple controls for heating and cooling systems (Photo courtesy of HAI).

consumer excited about the product line, but many have not sold well. Refrigerators with Internet connections aren't likely to be linked to the local grocery store, and the process of using such a device is so complicated that consumers are unwilling to spend money on it.

And money, after all, is everyone's bottom line.

Every Night at the Movies

8

There's no hiding one trend that's dominating the consumer electronics market these days: Big-screen and digital TVs are big. In the first 11 months of 2006, U.S. sales of plasma screen and LCD TVs jumped to 5 million sets, versus 941,000 during the same period in 2004, despite the fact that these televisions can run as high as $15,000 depending on the size and technology (plasma, LCD flat panel, or nonflat digital high-def).

From sleek plasma wall units that give new meaning to the phrase "reality TV" to hi-def consoles the size of washing machines, more is more. In addition, most television stations will continue broadcasting both analog and digital programming until February 17, 2009, when all analog broadcasting will stop. Analog TVs receiving over-the-air programming will still work after that date, but owners of these TVs will need to buy converter boxes to change digital broadcasts into analog format.

Converter boxes will be available from consumer electronics product retailers at that time. Cable and satellite subscribers with analog TVs will need to contact their service providers about obtaining converter boxes for the transition to digital television.

> To create the display on a plasma TV, tiny colored fluorescent lights are illuminated to form an image. Each pixel is made up of three fluorescent lights—a red light, a green, and a blue. The plasma display varies the intensities of the different lights to produce a full range of colors.

A 32-inch high-definition television brings theater quality viewing to the family room.

A flat screen hangs on a wall with a speaker above the screen and side speakers.

■ INSTALLING A TELEVISION

LCD and plasma screen televisions have changed our whole sense of how TVs fit in the house. For years, the trend was to design cabinets with doors to keep the televisions out of sight, much like you see in hotel rooms, but now, because newer TVs are generally lighter and slimmer, even over-sized floor units take up less space than their hulkier forebearers—and homeowners are opting to show them off. Some wall screens are so thin they're being hung like paintings. They're everywhere and can even be found hanging from soffits on kitchen counters.

> A 32-inch high-definition LCD television might range in price from about $800 to $3,500 depending on its manufacturer and features. Screens range from 15 to 65 inches.

Buying a big-screen TV is not necessarily a simple plug in and play proposition. Fitting the set you want into the home you have can raise a host of issues. Hanging a flat-panel TV on the wall, for example, is no big deal as long as there are identifiable wall studs that can take the weight. The big panels—61 to 63 inches—can weigh as much as 150 to 200 pounds.

Yet mounting a 65-pound flat panel on the wall is no small task, especially if you have to

The HDTV fits easily in existing space, such as this library/ viewing room.

drill into the brick-and-plaster wall and bolt the special mounting-bracket hanger that came with the set. If it is new construction and drywall, you can easily drill into the studs.

Big screens also can create sound issues. Owners need to consider the acoustics of the room, as well as how to isolate the big sound from the rest of the house (and the neighbors). Because the new sets pack such a powerful punch, some owners install extra-dense decorative panels on the walls in their entertainment room to reflect and focus the sound in a way that prevents distortion. To keep noise and any vibrations from the TV's sound system confined to a single room, you may need to install the kind of wall insulation originally designed to deaden noise from heating equipment.

> Plasma screen sizes start at 42 inches diagonal and range up to 61 inches, though screens as small as 37 inches and as large as 103 inches are available. Prices range from $1,500 to $15,000.

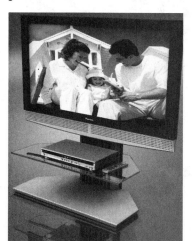

This flat-screen TV and accessories fits in a glass shelf that fits into a small space.

Is it all worth the trouble? No doubt about it, says Duane, the happy owner of a 54-inch Toshiba HD, which cost him $3,000. He was looking for an HDTV that would provide him with a going-to-the-movies experience. His television exceeds his expectations. He even watches the news, and can see every bit of the makeup the anchors are wearing.

■ HOME THEATERS

The new generation of LCDs and plasmas has added a large number of additional choices to creating a home theater. Under the category of home theater equipment also come DVD players, projection TVs, hi-fi stereo VCRs, and surround-sound processors. The basic components of a complete home theater package include a large-screen TV, a video source such as a VCR or DVD player, and audio electronics that control the whole system and create a surround-sound effect by using multiple speakers.

Many builders offer home theaters as options that can be financed in mortgage packages, which is not surprising because complete systems cost, on average, $3,500. Surveys have shown if given a choice between a theater, study, or bedroom for a 12-by-14-foot room off the family room, 57 percent of buyers would take the theater. The home theater could be offered in basements or second-floor bonus rooms as well.

A room in the basement remodel accommodates a traditional theater setup.

The home theater is something that many buyers are willing to wait for, and how long they are willing to wait is determined by how deep their pockets are. The interest appears to be greater among high-end buyers, although the technology is getting more affordable. It is all tied in with home security and upgraded whole-house wiring. Even if people aren't going to install a home theater now, they want the house to be wired to accommodate it.

Wiring is an issue. Most existing homes have Category 1 telephone wire, which is designed for voice communication. So-called smart-house wiring uses Category 5 data/communications wiring, which involves four twisted pair of wires instead of one.

This wiring moves data and voice signals quickly, which is especially important to buyers who plan to make heavy use of home offices. The Category 5 wiring is coupled with an upgraded coaxial TV cable that enables video signals to travel to television and computer monitors throughout the house.

Buyers in the Northeast who express an interest in such theaters focus on the basements, where most home theaters are located. In other areas of the country, such as the South and Southwest, where houses usually don't have basements, home theaters are on the first or second floors. Some experts lately are seeing a trend away from separate home theaters, which were common in the late 1980s and early 1990s. Instead, thanks to big-screen and high-definition television sets, the home theater is being

A Slingbox allows the user to pick up signals from a DVR on a computer anywhere by downloading software.

A Dell screen with side speakers.

Rather than a separate home theater, this system fits into a living room.

relegated to a smaller space in the family room rather than being in a room by itself. Parents have found that the kids stay in the home theater, and away from them.

To ensure crisp, larger-than-life screen images and full surround sound, cable or a digital satellite system is a must. Consider a DVD player, and replace your existing VCR with one with high-fidelity sound and a four-head video system.

Pick a screen large enough so that you will not be distracted by activities to the left and right

The amount of HDTV programming is increasing rapidly with HDTV broadcast, cable, and satellite service increasing in availability across the country. Also, the audio that is supplied with HDTV video is in surround sound, which takes further advantage of your surround-sound receiver.

of it. The rule is to buy a screen with a picture size, in inches, four to seven times the distance, in feet, from your screen to your seating position.

For surround sound, you need to select an audio/video receiver or surround processor that can decode the new digital audio systems and is compatible with tens of thousands of analog surround titles and television programs. Because surround processors provide six full channels of surround sound, having speakers that are matched at the three front channels

Speaker components cost about $1,200 and fit easily into small spaces.

The size of the television or video display device you get really depends on the size of the room environment you will be using it in and how close you will be sitting to the screen.

is essential. And don't forget to add a subwoofer, which is designed to produce bass.

The audio/video receiver is the heart of a home theater system and provides most, if not all, the inputs and outputs that you connect everything, including your television, into. An audio/video receiver provides an easy and cost-effective way of centralizing your home theater system. In many higher-end installations, the functions of an audio/video receiver are often provided by separate components of each channel. Such a setup provides more flexibility in switching out and/or upgrading the sepa-rate aspects of the system as well as isolating any interference that is caused by having all these functions combined in a single chassis and sharing the same power supply. For the average consumer, however, a good audio/video receiver will function just fine.

A rear projector for a real home theater setup.

A home theater in a box is a system that has all the components needed for a basic theater, including all speakers, a surround-sound receiver, and, most times, a DVD/CD player, and in a few cases, a DVD player and VCR combination or even a DVD recorder. If you are getting into home theater for the very first time and don't know what to get and how to set everything, a theater in a box may be a great way to get started.

A home theater in a box system starts at $200 but can go as high $2,000 or more.

Will and Ellen, TV junkies, were able to put a 51-inch HDTV that cost them $1,300 in the family room of their small house without much trouble. Ellen actually bought the television for Will's birthday in July, but gave it to him at Christmas.

"He expects his favorite team will be in the Super Bowl," Ellen said. "We're hoping that buying the TV means they will be."

More Do-It-Yourself Tips Online! **What do you need to create home theater? Find out at www.remodelingonthemoney.com**

Out the Door and in the Window

9

"The myth is that windows are where most heat is lost, but that is only because we spend time in areas where there are windows and we notice it more than anywhere else."

—**Liz Robinson, energy expert**

This is not an attempt to minimize the importance of windows and doors to the energy efficiency of a house. Instead, this is an effort to help you spend your money effectively. Energy efficiency requires a whole-house approach, not a piecemeal one. If you don't improve the insulation in the walls or air seal the gaps in the attic or basement, continue to use ancient appliances, and have to crank up your antique furnace to 90 degrees just to get the house to 60 in the dead of winter, spending gobs of money on windows and doors won't make a difference.

■ Fast Facts on Buying Windows

Check for strong, tight-fitting, sealed joints to prevent air and water leakage.

For windows that require thermal breaks, inspect a corner cutaway sample of the frame and the sash. Ensure that the exterior and interior surfaces are separated by an insulating material known as a thermal break.

For larger and heavier windows, ask if additional reinforcement is required and how this might affect the thermal performance.

■ WINDOWS

A window consists of a glazed unit, a frame, and a sash. The glazed unit fits into the sash, and the frame holds the sash. The frame and sash may occupy as much as one-third of the total window area. Both the frame and the sash can be major sources of heat loss. This heat loss is a result of conduction through the material. Heat loss also can result from air leakage, sometimes increased by expansion and contraction or warping of a window's frame or sashes.

A solid core front door is as beautiful from the inside as it is outside.

Highly conductive materials used in the construction of the frame and sash must have thermal breaks incorporated in order to reduce heat loss. A large amount of heat loss through the sash and frame will result in the formation of condensation and frost on interior window surfaces.

Two important ratings to check when buying windows and glazed doors are the R-value and the overall U-value. An R-value measures a material's resistance to heat transfer; the higher the R-value, the better the insulating properties of the glazing. The U-value measures overall energy efficiency. It tells you the rate at which heat flows through the entire window or door, frame and all. The lower the U-value, the more energy efficient the window or door. An average U-value is fine for warm climates; in cold climates, a lower U-value is worth the premium you are likely to pay for it.

Frames and sashes are manufactured from a variety of materials, such as aluminum, fiberglass, vinyl, and wood, or a combination of these materials. Each material has benefits and drawbacks in terms of insulating value, strength, durability, cost, aesthetics, and maintenance requirements.

Security issues have altered the function of windows in urban areas because, though windows are the eyes on the world, the world can see in also. Windows are locked, bolted, and barred, especially in crime-ridden neighborhoods. Instead of being the "eyes of the house," windows are considered weak points. Having to close them, however, robs a home's occupants of benefits such as cross ventilation and increases the use and cost of air-conditioning and fans.

Good-quality windows can be made using any of these materials.

How do you tell whether the windows are sound or will need to be replaced? Home inspectors recommend that each window be checked to see whether it operates as it was designed to. Sometimes windows in new construction have been installed too tightly, so they pinch the screens, which won't open and close easily. In older houses, the top sash has been painted shut because people rarely move it up and down.

The windows in very old or historic houses usually operate surprisingly well. Many owners of old houses like living in them and they have maintained the windows. Purists among the old-house owners often don't care about efficiency. Having leaky windows is a part of owning an old house. You can make them more efficient, but replacing them never even comes up.

To make older windows more efficient, homeowners strip and paint each sash, replace the glass and hardware, and install new weights and chains so that they move up and down easily. To compensate for their inefficiency, they seal gaps between the moving parts with weather stripping, or fill the gaps between the window frame and the wall with caulk. Storm windows often are installed to help reduce heat loss, and there are temporary fixes such as plastic film kits that create the effect of an interior storm window.

The return on replacement windows often varies within the same region. Location is still the most important factor. Aluminum or vinyl replacement windows would probably detract from Victorian-era houses, while in neighborhoods with newer houses, they truly could add value to the house.

Most wood windows come prehung in complete frames that fit into a rough opening in the wall. They are attached with nails driven through the exterior casing on the outside and through the jambs on the inside. Vinyl or aluminum windows and some wood windows with a vinyl or aluminum cladding have a factory-installed nailing flange on the outside that you attach to the perimeter of the window's rough framing.

How do you find leaks? Wet your fingertips and run them around the window frame to feel a draft.

Replacing windows improves the appearance and resale value of the home. It reduces maintenance costs such as painting, and makes cleaning easier with tilt-sash designs. It improves comfort by making the windows feel warmer in the winter or by cutting down unwanted solar heat in summer, and it reduces damage to furnishings by blocking ultraviolet light that can damage fabrics and other materials.

■ Fast Facts on Window Frames

Aluminum frames are strong and durable, maintain strength, offer low maintenance, and resist warping. Aluminum frames and sashes must be designed with thermal breaks to reduce conduction heat loss.

Fiberglass rates high in energy performance. In some designs, the hollow sections of the frame and sash are filled with foam insulation to further decrease heat loss. Fiberglass frames offer good structural strength and durability and require minimal maintenance.

Wood frames have a good insulating value and structural strength but require protection from the weather. Low-maintenance, factory-applied claddings and finishes are available. They must prevent water from becoming trapped behind them. Look for well-sealed corners as well as gaskets between the cladding and the glazing. Heat-conductive cladding materials should not touch the glazing or extend in from the outside of the window toward the interior. When installed in this manner, they can cause condensation problems and lower the thermal performance of the window.

Extruded vinyl frames provide good thermal performance and are easy to maintain. Large vinyl windows may be reinforced to increase their strength; some reinforcing materials may increase conductive heat loss.

Thermally welded corners can prevent air and water leakage if the welds are continuous. Hollow sections of vinyl frames can be filled with foam insulation to improve thermal performance.

A window may be divided into one or more sashes, some of which may move and others that may be fixed. For example, a double-hung window generally has two moveable sashes, while a single-hung window has just one moveable sash. A sash may be divided into two or more lights (panes of glass) held in place by mullions and muntins.

The combination window frame or sash combines two or more materials, such as aluminum, fiberglass, wood, and vinyl. The objective is to obtain the best features of each material so that the frame and sash will provide good thermal performance, durability, and strength, and require minimal maintenance.

Combination windows use different materials separately in appropriate areas, while windows made out of composite materials have frames and sashes made out of materials such as fiberglass and wood that have been "blended" together through a manufacturing process. Composite materials essentially adopt the positive attributes of the materials from which they are made in a single unified form.

Window shopping? Download an e-book on what you need to look for at www.remodelingonthemoney.com

Vic lives in a turn-of-the-20th-century "vernacular" house, which means that the architect designed something that took in various aspects of old and contemporary styles popular at the time. The three front windows on the first floor of the three-story semi-detached house were totally inefficient and no amount of tweaking, including the addition of aluminum storm windows, would make them less leaky in the winter.

Vic hired a window company to replace the three windows with vinyl ones that looked very much like the original windows in the showroom, but that needed considerable retrofitting to make them look as if they belonged with the rest of the house. Each of the windows cost $500, but in the end, the effort succeeded. Not only did the three new windows look as if they belonged, but the living room, still in the shadows during the winter, was much warmer after they were installed. Replacing the remaining 20 windows, however, at $500 each, was out of the question so Vic tried to make those as energy efficient as possible.

There are two types of windows: those that open, or are operable, and those that don't, or are fixed. Experts recommend using as many fixed windows as codes allow, keeping in mind that floors with bedrooms need at least one operable window for emergency exit. Fixed windows are more efficient because of their better air-tightness characteristics. They also offer the most safety and security.

Of the operable units, there are many forms: awning, casement, hopper, horizontal slider, vertical slider (either single' or double hung), and turn and tilt. There are two ways of sealing operable windows to minimize air leakage: with a compression or a sliding seal. Windows with compression

Condensation can be decreased or eliminated by raising the inside surface temperature and/or decreasing the relative humidity of the indoor air. Energy-efficient windows are least likely to have condensation. Their resistance to condensation, however, depends on the indoor humidity level. A humidity level of more than 40 percent, when the outside temperature is –5 degrees or colder, may cause condensation even on a well-performing window.

Because new windows can be very expensive, experts recommend replacing leaky windows gradually—starting with the most uncomfortable room in the house.

Glazing is the generic term for the transparent or translucent material in a window or door.

Make sure that warm air from furnace vents doesn't flow directly onto the interior surface of the window glass, because this could give rise to thermal stress problems in the glazed unit and could cause the glass to break.

Latches on the frame are used to hold the window tightly closed. On hinged windows, two are recommended on tall or wide frames. On double-hung windows, sash locks pull together the upper and lower sash to minimize drafts. Keyed sash locks can improve security. On sliders, look for security locks to keep the operable sashes from being jimmied open.

Weather stripping has improved over the past 20 years. More durable, better performing plastic weather stripping is used in most ENERGY STAR–qualified windows.

seals are generally the more airtight of operable types and should be the window of choice whenever possible. Casement, awning, hopper, and turn-and-tilt windows, for example, should have a closure/locking mechanism that pulls the unit tight against the seal. Make sure the gasket is a compression, neoprene rubber type.

Sometimes, the decision to replace windows in an older house doesn't rest solely with the homeowner. In historic districts, there are rules governing replacement windows. Whatever changes you make to the exterior of your house are governed by those rules, and even if the windows you want are more efficient than what you have now, you have to comply with what the historic commission wants.

Jim's addition required historic wood windows specific to the municipality that matched those in the rest of the house. He sent his contractor to one of the local companies that made the historic windows and the contractor obtained ones that matched the sizes and look of the origi-

nals. They were single rather than double pane, as most new energy-efficient windows are, but because they were correctly installed in the openings with the proper flashing, the walls and frames around the windows were properly insulated to the standards of the region. Jim notes that "they are as tight and as efficient as windows in any new house."

In contrast, Pam had brand-new energy-efficient windows installed in her new house, and every one of them leaked like a sieve—not only cold air in the winter, but water during heavy

Sliding windows add much to the look of a room.

rainstorms. On windy days, you couldn't keep a candle lighted in front of them, and Pam's heating bills went through the roof. Finally, a carpenter was called in to reinstall the windows, which he did properly, and a roofer replaced the gutters above the windows, which had been hung improperly. The heating bills were cut in half.

> The biggest test of the energy efficiency of a replacement window is the gas, electric, or oil bill for the following year.

There are a lot of high-performance wood windows on the market that satisfy local historic commissions. Andersen, Pella, WeatherShield, and Marvin have products that will meet those needs.

For example, when REALTOR®/developer Mark Wade tackled the "model-Remodel" house for the 1999 Remodelers Show, he found that the original win-

Modern windows tilt in for easy cleaning.

dows were no good, but that the frames and trim merely had to be stripped and repainted. WeatherShield supplied the 17 windows, which fit perfectly in the openings and allowed Mark to keep the look of a 19th-century house. The glass was insulated, and the windows, which fit tightly into those frames, were energy efficient.

We often blame the windows themselves for our energy problems, but much of the heat is lost in the space around the windows. Cold air can find its way in through the gap where the bottom edge of a windowsill meets the wall, and a little dab of caulk will fix it, so it might be wise to look at whatever you decide on the windows within the context of the entire house.

The National Park Service suggests that before you decide what to do about windows in historic homes, try to understand the contribution of the windows to the appearance of the facade, including the pattern of the openings and their size, the proportions of the frame and sash, the configuration of windowpanes, muntin profiles, the type of wood, paint color, characteristics

> One problem with replacing windows in older houses is that they are often odd sized. Before World War II, there was no universal construction standard, so builders made windows in sizes unique to that house.

Learn how to turn "low-e" into lower heating and cooling costs at www.remodelingonthemoney.com

associated details such as arched tops, hoods, or other decorative elements.

Develop an understanding of how the window reflects the period, style, or regional character-istics of the building, or represents technological development. Armed with an awareness of the signifi-cance of the existing window, begin to search for a replacement that retains as much of the character of the historic window as possible.

In new construction, standard windows are not that expensive com-pared with the total cost of the house. However, special windows, such as transoms, half moons, and Palla-dian, add a considerable amount to the cost. Builders estimate that win-dows constitute 3 percent of the sales price of a typical new home. For a $300,000, 3,200-square-foot house, that means $9,000. Divide that by 25 standard windows, and you are talking $360 a window.

Vinyl windows, which are common in new construction, are less expensive than wood

Simonton windows are full-size, but open like skylights (Photo courtesy of Simonton).

Proper window installation should include wall repair.

ones. The price difference between the two is typically about $60, but price should not be the sole deciding factor. Window experts say that most people who want replacement windows really don't know what the windows are supposed to do or aren't really up on the latest advances in energy efficiency. They come into showrooms expecting windows to do more than they are designed to do and go away disappointed.

A lot of homebuyers and homeown-ers don't like the look of vinyl, no matter how maintenance-free vinyl windows are, so manufacturers and builders offer wooden windows or ones that have vinyl on the outside and wood inside.

Energy-Efficient Windows

Efficient windows are much more widely available than they were a decade ago, thanks to the rapid growth of new technologies. Double-pane windows with low-emissivity (low-E) coating can reduce heating bills by 34 percent in cold climates, compared with uncoated, single-pane windows.

Standard window glass easily allows the sun's energy to pass through it. However, at night, it is equally effective at emitting infrared heat energy back through it to the exterior through the process known as radiative heat loss. This *high-emissivity* characteristic of conventional glazing has led researchers to develop low-E coatings.

A low-E coating is a thin, invisible metallic layer—only several atoms in thickness—applied directly to glazing surfaces. In a typical double-pane application, the low-E coating is normally applied to the exterior face of the interior glazing. While it is transparent to short-wave solar energy, it is opaque to long-wave infrared energy. What this means is that a low-E coating allows most of the sun's solar spectrum (including visible light) to pass through the window to the interior, but the coating reflects most heat energy (from room temperature objects) back to its source, which is a benefit both in the winter, because it keeps the heat in, and in the summer, because it keeps out the heat radiated from warm objects outside.

A low-E coating on one pane in a double-glazed window can give the window an insulating value about the same as a standard triple-glazed unit, without the added weight of a third glazing. The lower weight reduces wear and tear on the window's hinges, casement cranks, and the like, making it easier to operate and giving the window longer life. It also reduces transportation costs, which means lower prices. There is usually some loss of solar contribution due to the low-E coating, but while this reduces the benefits of passive solar heat gains somewhat, it is more than offset by the improved insulative value of the low-E window at night. An added bonus is that fewer ultraviolet rays make it through,

Window walls, if properly installed, let in plenty of light but allow little heat transfer.

which can mean less fading of carpets and fabric.

The other big advance in window technology has been the introduction of inert gas fills into the space between glazings. Inert means chemically stable and safe gases. Argon and krypton are the usual choice, with argon being the most common and cheapest. Filling the space between glazing layers with argon gas reduces heat loss through conduction because argon has low conductivity and reduces convection losses, and because it is

Skylights have automatic shutters that open and close at the push of a button.

■ Fast Facts on Low-Emissivity Coatings

High solar-gain, low-E coatings allow as much heat from the sun to enter the house as clear glass. High solar-gain coatings offer the greatest energy savings in regions with cool summers and very cold winters.

Moderate solar-gain, low-E coatings screen a portion of the sun's heat, keeping the home cooler in summer but admitting a good amount of solar heat in winter. They offer the greatest energy savings in regions with moderately hot summers and cold winters.

Low solar-gain, low-E coatings screen the most heat from the sun. They offer the greatest energy savings in regions with very hot summers and either cold or mild winters. By blocking ultraviolet radiation, these coatings also reduce fading of furniture, floor coverings, artwork, and window treatments.

During the winter, the sun's low elevation in the sky at midday enables it to shine through south-facing windows. These solar gains can help reduce your heating costs during the winter.

heavier than air and prevents gas from moving between the glazings. Krypton performs a bit better than argon and allows the space between the panes to be smaller, which reduces the amount of costly gas and allows multiple-pane systems with less chance of breakage because of stress.

Low-E coatings are also applied to thin sheets of transparent polyester and suspended in the cavity between glazings or directly on the glass surface. This combines a high solar transmission with a low emissivity. Some films are designed to combine low emissivity with reduced solar transmission, making them ideal for Southern climates or west-facing windows if solar gains are a severe problem during the summer.

Skylights are perfect for lighting up dark upper floor rooms.

Single-, double-, or triple-glazed refer to the number of panes of glass incorporated into the window unit: single-glazed is one pane; double-glazed, two panes; and triple-glazed, three panes. Energy-efficient windows are double-glazed at minimum. To determine the number of glazings in a particular window, hold a light next to the glass and count the reflections. In a double-glazed window, you'll see two main reflections, corresponding to the number of glazings.

Most window manufacturers offer several types of glazing, which affect the insulation value of the window and the likelihood of condensation forming on the glass. Sometimes, transparent plastic films are placed inside the glazing unit between the panes of glass to increase energy efficiency. A variety of coatings on the glazing surfaces, such as plastic films or inert gases between glazings, for example, can increase the insulating value of a double-glazed window to

■ Fast Facts on Energy-Efficient Windows

New windows should meet the following guidelines:

They should have low-E coatings, which let in visible light but block radiant heat losses to cut heating bills.

They should have solar control, or "spectrally-selective," coatings to block solar heat gain to save cooling energy but let in visible light.

The windows should have insulated frames. Metal frames without insulation are the least efficient. Vinyl, insulated vinyl, fiberglass, and wood frames are more efficient.

The invisible gas filler in a double-pane window is critical to energy efficiency. Instead of plain air, high-efficiency models use argon or krypton gas, which conducts very little heat and helps the window's insulating properties.

The material used to create the separation between the two panes of glass, called a thermal break, was traditionally metal. New materials are better insulating and make the overall window more efficient.

In a warm climate, retrofit films can be applied to windows to reduce solar gain and cut cooling costs.

> Overheating in summer tends to occur more from unshaded west-facing windows and, to a lesser extent, east windows. Well-placed deciduous trees will reduce summer overheating while permitting desirable winter solar gains.

> Most of the air leakage of operable windows occurs between the window's sash and frame or at the meeting rails of a sliding sash.

more than equal that of a standard triple-glazed window. Coatings are often used with gas fill.

Most windows now incorporate sealed, insulated glazing units in which two or more glazing layers are sealed around the outside edge to prevent air or moisture from entering the air space, eliminating dirt and condensation between glazings. If moist air finds its way into the sealed air space, condensation may form between the glazings. This is usually caused by a faulty seal and cannot be corrected except by replacing the insulated glazing unit.

Between the windowpanes in a conventional double-glazed window where the glass meets the frame, you will probably see a strip of material, known as a spacer. The purpose of spacers is to maintain a uniform separation between the panes of glass. They have traditionally been made of hollow aluminum, containing a drying agent or desiccant designed to absorb the initial moisture present at the time of manufacture in the space between the glazings.

The insulated glazing unit is held in the sash using various sealing methods to prevent water from entering the interface between the glass unit and the sash. Check the sealing system on both the interior and the exterior surfaces for an effective continuous seal. Trapped water in the sash is probably the greatest cause of failure of the glazing unit. Some manufacturers incorporate a drainage system into the sash; this feature allows any water that may otherwise be trapped to drain away.

A price and quality comparison is essential. Low-priced, poor-quality windows are not a good, long-term investment. Energy-efficient, durable, low-maintenance windows will provide energy savings, increase comfort levels, reduce or eliminate condensation on the interior surface of windows, and last longer.

Style in a glass kitchen door.

Even closet doors merit good treatment, especially if it's on the first floor near the entry.

Metal spacers conduct energy easily and are a significant source of heat loss and poor window performance. The best insulating spacers are often made from nonmetallic materials. There are also hybrid spacers made out of metal and nonmetallic materials. These materials do not conduct nearly as much heat.

■ DOORS

Doors have less impact than windows on the energy consumption of a home—unless they are patio or garden doors—simply because there are fewer of them. They come in a variety of materials, some of which reduce heat flow better than others. Depending on style and insulation material, for example, metal-clad doors are more efficient than solid wooden doors.

No matter what the material, ill-fitting doors lose even more energy and can make the home drafty and uncomfortable.

Heat may be lost through the door and frame; between the door, frame, and sill; through glass in patio doors

> Hinged French doors with a center post to close against will be more airtight as patio doors than the sliding variety.

or doors with windows; and between the door frame and rough frame opening. Heat loss through doors can be reduced through careful choice of the door, its location, and proper installation and maintenance. You can reduce heat loss simply by placing a door out of the path of prevailing winds, by locating it on the leeward side of a house, or by providing windbreaks. Another option is the use of an airlock vestibule that traps the

Traditional style doors are available for period renovations.

air between the exterior door and the interior of the house.

Exterior French doors must have a center frame for tightness.

The front door of an Arts-and-Crafts-style house is a reproduction of that style by Classic Craft (Photo courtesy of Classic Craft).

Missing or worn weather stripping, improperly located strike plates, frames that no longer fit the door correctly, or warped doors that no longer contact the stops are the main contributors to air leakage. These problems can all be corrected by a carpenter or competent do-it-yourselfer. A badly deteriorated door should be replaced with a new one with energy-efficient insulation. Select good-quality units and install them properly.

New insulated doors are usually made of foam and wood covered with metal. Door frames are normally wood, clad with metal or vinyl. Doors that are mainly glass and are used as windows should be compared for energy performance. Glass inserts and sidelights should have at least double glazing with at least one-half inch of air space between glazings and be compared on the basis of the U-value or R-value calculated for the complete door system.

Patio doors can range in width from 5- to 12-feet wide. The most popular patio doors are sliding glass and French doors.

Sliding glass doors are typically very large panes of glass mounted in a frame with rollers. They come in a variety of materials including aluminum, which is the least expensive and won't rust; vinyl, which is low maintenance and energy efficient with low-E glass and weather stripping installed in the factory; wood, which is typically the highest quality and most expensive; and wood clad, which is a wooden door and frame with vinyl, fiberglass, or aluminum coating on the exterior. They give you an energy-efficient outdoor coating and real wood indoors.

■ Fast Facts on Doors

Steel doors have energy-efficient foam-core insulation and are fully weather-stripped by the manufacturer. They are highly resistant to shrinking, swelling, and warping. Their tough steel construction will withstand years of extreme weather conditions with minimum maintenance. The doors can be purchased with predrilled doorknob and lockset holes, making installation even easier. Steel doors come preprimed and ready to paint.

Fiberglass doors offer the same energy-saving and easy installation qualities as steel doors. Fiberglass doors have wood-grain texture molded into the door, so they give the appearance of a real wood door when painted or stained. Their high-quality composite construction makes these doors resistant to all sorts of weather as well as scratches and dents. These are an excellent choice for extreme climates and high-traffic entrances.

Wood doors offer the most traditional look. The familiar look and feel of a well-crafted wooden door sends an inviting message of home and hearth. The substantial weight of a wooden door adds a sense of security and sturdiness to your home. These doors may be painted or stained for a natural, warm appearance. Wooden doors are usually made using frame and panel construction to counteract the effects of climatic or seasonal changes.

An in-swing door opens inward; an out-swing door opens outward.

A light is a pane of glass in a door; divided lights are panes of glass that are or appear to be divided. A grille is an assembly fitted into the door that gives the appearance of divided lights.

An etched glass entry door hearkens back to another time.

French doors are available in the same materials as sliding glass doors and more. They are also available in steel and fiberglass, with the same characteristics as those found in traditional entry doors of the same material. French doors are available with either left- or right-handed in swing or out swing.

Hap created a "passive solar hallway" designed to reduce energy consumption by 20 percent using low-E glass doors. The hallway was part of an addition that allowed Hap to use the arched opening, through which horses and carriage passed when his house was a stable, as the entrance to the living room instead.

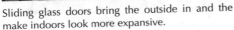
Sliding glass doors bring the outside in and the make indoors look more expansive.

French doors add panache to any room.

The south-facing hallway has tile floors to capture and hold heat. It has large eaves—and 22 deciduous trees—to shade the space in the summer. The all-electric house has central air-conditioning but, according to Hap, "it is rarely used, and then only to reduce the humidity level in the house." A whole-house fan provides 99 percent of the cooling needed in the summer.

A month before his wedding day, Hap had ordered eight-foot-high glass doors and windows to fill the space to create the hallway. The supplier sent six-foot, eight-inch units instead, and it was too late to order new ones. Hap filled the space above with transom windows as a landscaper was installing the concrete patio in front of the addition and another man was setting up the tent for the outdoor wedding.

"Everyone finished on time, and the wedding went on without a hitch," he said.

Notes from the Underground

> ❝No dry basement is dry all the time.❞
>
> **—Jim McAleer, veteran builder**

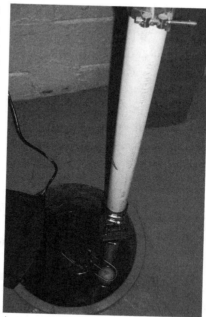

10

That's what Frank found out, much to his surprise, early one autumn morning, when he went down the stairs to his basement to retrieve something he'd left there the night before. The less-than-a-year-old, wall-to-wall carpet was covered in two inches of water, flowing from sumps on either side of the basement.

"The flooding could have been worse," Frank said. "We have two sump pumps that work in tandem in separate pits, and both decided to die at once. Fortunately, I was able to catch the problem before the water reached the furnace and the washer and dryer, and quickly install replacement pumps that rapidly lowered the water level."

Even in heavy rains on top of melting snow left by a blizzard, Frank's basement had remained dry as a bone with no evidence of moisture where the basement

A sump pump in a pit in a basement. The plastic splash block carries water from a drain hole in a dehumidifier collection well so that the well never has to be emptied.

walls and floor met. Fully confident that any severe moisture problem had been licked, he and his wife, Nancy, decided to create a recreation room with a big-screen television set for their two sons and their friends to hang out in. When they decided to carpet the floor of the rec room, they chose a carpet that resisted mold and mildew so cleaning and drying the damp portion of the rug took little time. To be on the safe side, Frank called the gas company to check out the furnace for possible water damage. There was none.

When people buy older houses, one of the first questions they ask is whether the basement is wet or dry. Although a finished basement is just one item on a buyer's wish list, it sometimes can make or break a resale.

"It seems that most buyers have one column for needs and one column for wants, and the finished basement appears first on the wants column," one real estate broker says. "Buyers are looking for basements that have outside access and daylight. In new homes, basements with doors that open into the backyard are extremely popular."

■ Fast Facts on Sump Pumps

Sump pumps typically range from one-third to one-half horsepower and can pump 2,200 to 3,000 gallons every hour.

Depending on their capacity, they may require their own circuit because an overload breaking a circuit could rob you of the pump as the water is rising.

Consider a battery backup for the pump or even a generator that can operate the unit in the event of a prolonged power outage. Backup pumps can cost more than the one already in place and often require enlarging the sump to accommodate both.

Expect to spend $150 to $500 for a pump, depending on features and size. If your present pump is more than 20 years old, the plumber will likely have to retrofit it to the discharge pipe. You can install more than one pump if your flooding problem is severe.

Consider installing a water monitor near the sump pit that will sound when the water on the floor reaches a certain level. They typically work on nine-volt batteries that should be replaced every six months.

The water leading toward the sump must be filtered through gravel and drain tile in order to minimize silting up of the system. The sump must be located in the lowest spot of the basement or crawlspace.

The sump and sump pump should be covered.

You CAN work around moisture issues to create basement living space.
Find out how at www.remodelingonthemoney.com

■ REMOVING WATER FROM YOUR BASEMENT

When Dick and Pam bought their house from the investors who had rehabbed it, they noticed that, unlike every other house in their neighborhood, their basement had no water management system—not even the minimum sump pit and pump. The floor of the basement, covered with gray basement paint, looked fresh and unmarred. There was no evidence of mold and mildew, so they thought that, for some reason, they had lucked out on a dry basement.

Water control and management in the crawlspace is essential for maintaining a house. The most common problem associated with wet crawlspaces is that moist conditions can lead to wood-destroying fungus that deteriorates exposed framing.

About the same time they were considering converting part of the basement into a bedroom for their three older sons, a storm brought several inches of rain, and water began rising through the basement floor. Fortunately, they had not stored anything directly on the floor, so damage was minimal, and the furnace was raised far enough above the floor to escape damage.

A perimeter drain has been cut where the basement wall meets the concrete floor to allow moisture to be channeled to the sump pit.

The couple hired a contractor to create a sump pit and drainage so they could proceed with their bedroom plans. The contractor picked a spot near the back wall so that the water the pump expels could exit the basement and continue on 10 feet or more outside and well away from the foundation.

Once the sump pump was installed, there was no further flooding in the basement during heavy rains, and the bedroom for the boys was completed, including a large walk-in closet for clothes and toys. While most homeowners are looking for a spot outside the basement for the laundry room, Amy decided to keep the washer and dryer close by the boys' rooms to make her life easier.

As you can easily see, moisture remains a major issue for basement renovation, and because "down under" is one of the places first-time buyers on tight budgets consider for expansion

Basement moisture collected in the sump is carried through a PVC pipe, which is usually about two inches in diameter, to the yard or through the front yard to the gutter along the street. Most municipalities prohibit a sump pump from connecting to the soil line, but in those communities where it is allowed, a backflow valve must be installed where the sump pipe and the soil line connect to prevent waste from backing up into the sump pit.

DAP's Kwik Seal-Plus Basement Paint with Microban, is popular because it is both latex-based and lower in odor than comparable paints. Microban is an antimicrobial agent also used in socks, tubs, and cutting boards. The paint comes with a guarantee that includes resistance of up to five pounds per square inch of water pressure. Price: 1-gallon can, $24.99; 3.5-gallon container, $79.99.

Home theaters and recreation rooms for children generate lots of noise. Consider installing soundproofing or a noise-reduction system between the walls of those specialty rooms and the floors.

as the family grows, the issue needs to be tackled in a more-than-satisfactory way. Sometimes the problem is taken care of easily, simply by purchasing a dehumidifier designed to keep the humidity levels in the basement relatively low— a recommendation of 40 percent is considered low enough to reduce the possibility of mold and mildew growth.

Basement waterproofing is designed to make the space mold-proof. Wichita-based Koch Waterproofing's Tuff-N-Dri product consists of spraying on a polymer-modified asphalt emulsion, then protecting it with an inorganic fiber insulation/drainage board. Finally, one-inch extruded polystyrene is applied to the inside of basement walls for enough permeability to allow wet areas to dry out before mold forms.

The roles basements play these days are similar to the ones they have played since at least the mid-1950s with the birth of the "rumpus room"—a lot of parents are finishing them for their teenagers so that the parents can have the family room to themselves while encouraging their children to stay at home for recreation. That's what Frank and Nancy did, and, despite the surprise demise of two sump pumps on the same day, they have had no regrets about the decision.

Dick and Pam aren't the only people who have targeted the basement as a bedroom for their children. When Richard and Joan were in the market for a house for seven children, bedroom space was a premium. Fortunately, they were able to find a house with a basement that could

(Left) A moisture barrier is installed on the interior of the basement at a point where there is a possibility of contact with the damp ground.

(Right) A dehumidifier keeps moisture levels in the basement at a level that won't result in mold and mildew growth.

Checking drawer alignment in a kitchen base cabinet before installation.

Installing the face frame on a base cabinet.

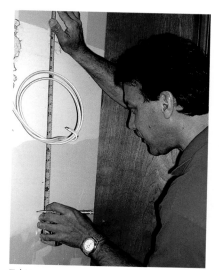

Taking measurements on the wall for vent-hood installation.

Using a drywall saw to make cuts for vent-hood installation.

Aligning the plywood base on which the hood will be centered and installed.

Lifting the cherry wood hood in place on the base.

Measuring a cut on a sheet of drywall for installation.

Making sure that the tile is aligned to the chalk line that designates the center of the room.

Snapping another chalk line from the center line on which the tiles will be aligned.

Using a notched trowel to spread the adhesive on which the tile will be laid.

Fitting a tile into the adhesive.

Making sure a row of tile is correctly aligned. One mistake and the tile would be off.

Adhesive is cleaned from the surface of the tile with a sponge before the adhesive dries.

Making sure the grout lines are even.

Edging tile is measured for the tile floor.

Edging tile is trimmed to fit on a wet saw.

Measuring a cut on a sheet of drywall for installation.

A window frame is trimmed before a window is installed (Simonton Windows).

A window is installed in a frame with one worker working on the inside and another, outside.

Trim is installed after a window installation.

Scrap wood is used to see where the base trim will be the side.

Adjustments are made to the side trim using a piece of scrap wood.

The window opening is measured carefully before the trim is installed.

Vinyl is cut in sections for the creation of windows (Simonton Windows).

Acrylic spray is used to revitalize an old bathtub.

The excess acrylic is peeled away from the tile surrounding the tub after installation.

Framing the roof of an addition.

Cabinet doors are sanded on an assembly line in a KraftMaid plant in Ohio (Photo courtesy of KraftMaid).

Quality control of cabinet doors on the KraftMaid assembly line.

A two-story addition and a garage are added to an existing house.

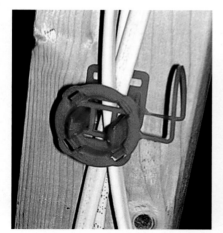

Code requires that all electrical wiring be collected behind the wall.

To prevent leaks from ice damming on a roof, a rubber membrane manufactured by W. R. Grace is installed.

■ Fast Facts on Dehumidifiers

Most basements cannot handle the summer without a dehumidifier; they come in sizes ranging from 30 pints to 65 pints.

Dehumidifiers remove moisture from the air by cooling it, causing it to condense on coils and be collected in a container in the machine for disposal. Reducing the moisture creates inhospitable living conditions for dust mites and mold.

According to the Association of Home Appliance Manufacturers, a moderately damp, 1,500-square-foot basement area should have a dehumidifier capable of removing 18 pints of water from the air every 24 hours.

Buy an energy-efficient model that allows you to set the humidistat to the desired humidity level, and make sure you empty it when it is full. Many can be drained directly into the sump with a hose, so you will not have to worry.

A typical dehumidifier can use anywhere from 50 to 200 watts, and if it runs for long periods, it can really rack up the electric bill. That is one good reason for buying a model with a humidistat because the machine will only come on and stay on for as long as it takes to get the relative humidity to the preset level, much as a thermostat on furnace does. That's also a reason why the dehumidifier you buy should be ENERGY STAR rated.

If you are putting a dehumidifier in a cold crawlspace, make sure that the machine is capable of operating properly when the ambient air falls to low temperatures. Some special dehumidifiers can operate at temperatures as low as freezing.

Make sure that you clean the dehumidifier filter regularly. Some models come with the warning lights that let you know when the filter is dirty.

Price: $150 to $400.

accommodate a bedroom for their two sons. Unfortunately, the housing development was built in an apple orchard, and during a rainstorm one night a few weeks after the family moved in, the basement filled with several inches of water, which one of the boys discovered on his way to the bathroom. The water drained quickly, but the carpet in the boys' room had to be removed and replaced with linoleum. The couple sued the developer, who, while not acknowledging he was at fault, paid to have a drainage system installed and the foundation waterproofed.

Being at the lowest point of the house, basements bear the brunt of any immediate increase in water. Typically, many homeowners don't have low-cost, federally guaranteed flood insurance to cover the damage if the house isn't in

The typical basement lets in *18 gallons of moisture each day.* As the dehumidifier removes the moisture, it makes room for more.

the required municipally designated flood zone or if the mortgage company doesn't require it.

Sharon and Todd faced that issue during heavy rains that pushed the river at the edge of their backyard over its banks and into their house. The floor of the basement was mostly dirt, with only the furnace located on a piece of concrete. They lost the furnace, although much of the damage, including pumping out of the floodwater, was handled for free by

Two-by-two foot panels—wood on the top and corrugated plastic on the bottom are installed as a basement subfloor over concrete. The plastic keeps the cold and damp below the floor (Photo courtesy of SubFlor Advance).

Before the rainy season arrives, make sure your sump pump works. Use the check valve to test it. If there is no water in the pump, pour some in to make sure it works.

the state environmental protection department. The furnace was not covered, however. The couple had no idea that the house was in a designated flood zone, and the mortgage company, which should have known and required them to get low-cost coverage from the National Flood Insurance Program administered by the Federal Emergency Management Agency, declined to take responsibility for replacing the furnace.

■ CREATING A DRY BASEMENT

In new houses, with all the waterproofing and construction techniques now available, building a dry basement is easier than ever, and that has led to the growing demand by owners of older houses for the same thing. The problem is, before World War II, older houses were not built with the idea that the basement

Floor joists made of engineered wood are used for an addition over a crawlspace (Photo courtesy of Boise Cascade).

would be used as expansion space. Many builders used concrete-block foundations that were porous, and lately have been shifting to poured concrete and interlocking concrete forms—both of which are much less porous than concrete block.

■ Fast Facts on Cleaning Up a Basement After a Flood

Q: How do I get rid of the smell after a flood at my house?

A: After removing water and mud with a broom or wet-dry vacuum, spray surfaces with lukewarm water, starting with the floor then moving to the walls and working up. Use a coarse brush or long-handled broom to scrub these surfaces.

Next, use hot water with a heavy-duty cleaner to scrub all surfaces, again from the bottom to the top. Follow with a rinse using a brush moistened with a solution of two tablespoons of chlorine bleach per gallon of water. Repeat scrubbing and rinsing until the odor is gone. Don't open the windows if it is humid. Buy or rent a dehumidifier, or run central air-conditioning or fans to dry things out.

Q: How do I disinfect after water and sewage come in?

A: Use a solution of one part chlorine bleach to nine parts water, especially if the water has sewage in it. You can use rock salt on hard surfaces, such as plaster and painted drywall, but not on concrete floors, which the salt will damage. Use one cup of rock salt per gallon of water. Never mix bleach and ammonia; hazardous fumes result.

Q: What about wet carpeting?

A: If a carpet has been soaked with water and sewage, ditch it. You'll never be able to clean it, and it's a health risk. When you pick it up, use rubber gloves, and be careful not to scrape your skin to avoid infection.

If the water damage is slight, remove the carpet—if it's not glued down—roll it up and take it outside. Drape it over a sawhorse or chairs so it will drain, but do not let it dry this way or it can stretch out of shape. Once the water drains, lay the carpet on the ground to finish drying. Get rid of the carpet pad. Wash floors as described above.

Have the carpet cleaned professionally or rent a steam cleaner. If the carpet must stay in place, use a wet-dry vacuum to clean up mud and water. Some experts suggest using liquid (but not full strength) ammonia cleaner or pine-based cleaner, but make sure these will not stain the carpet or cause it to fade. Be sure the carpet is dry before bringing it inside. Residual moisture can breed mildew and mold.

Q: How do I dry out walls and floors?

A: If the walls are insulated, you may need to remove the baseboards to ventilate wall cavities. Unless moisture there is allowed to dry, odors will linger. After you have removed the baseboards, drill holes a few inches above the floor between the studs to drain water. The insulation might have to be removed, dried, and replaced. Wet insulation is useless, can breed mold and mildew, and will perpetually stink.

Plastered walls and washable vinyl wallpaper can be cleaned. Allow the plaster to dry thoroughly before washing it. Use a mild soap and water to clean painted walls. If you have to repaint, wait a couple months for the walls to dry completely or the new paint will

(*Continued*)

■ Fast Facts on Cleaning Up a Basement After a Flood (*Continued*)

blister. Woodwork should be cleaned with a stiff brush and nonsudsing detergent while the wood is still wet. Wood floors will buckle, so leave them alone to dry. Open doors and windows on nonhumid days, and maintain an indoor temperature of about 55 degrees or the wood will warp or shrink. On warm days, use fans or air conditioners.

Q: What about the furnace?

A: Any heating system exposed to flooding needs to be checked. Even if it works, the chimney and smoke box could be clogged with dirt, and the furnace could explode. Check the part of the chimney that meets the foundation to ensure the water has not washed away mortar. If you use fuel oil, inspect the storage tank for opened seams. Do not turn on the fan motor or electric-ignition system unless they are clean and dry. Have all heating systems checked by competent repair people, preferably those who usually do service for you. If you must turn the heat on soon, keep it low. High heat will dry out wood floors too fast and cause them to warp.

Q: How do I dry out important papers and photographs?

A: First, drain water from the items by placing them upright in a box, separated by wax paper. Stand up books vertically on their spines. If photos are stuck together, don't pull them apart. Wet them again, then try it so you don't damage the emulsion. Clean photos carefully in a photo tray and put them between clean blotters to absorb the water, changing the blotters frequently. Put the documents in plastic freezer bags and store them in the freezer until you are ready to deal with them. Freezing delays further damage from mildew. To dry photos, hang them on a clothesline or run a fan to let air circulate over them.

The moisture problem must be solved before any remodeling can be done, and before you can correct or manage the moisture problem, you'll need to locate the source.

The problems can range from high levels of humidity to the entry of liquid water, resulting in mildew, water damage, rotting components and structural problems, and health effects. Rainwater is one of the most prevalent causes of basement moisture; the solution is to direct it away from the foundation because the foundation is not designed

QuietZone acoustic insulation batts manufactured by Owens Corning are being installed in interior basement walls to deaden sound (Photo courtesy of Owens Corning).

to be watertight. Other common sources include the entry of warm, humid outdoor air into the cool basement, high groundwater levels beneath the building, and plumbing leaks. A back-drafting furnace or an unvented clothes dryer also can contribute to basement moisture.

Rainwater is not supposed to pool near the foundation, but often does in rainstorms. Regrading will be necessary; landscapers recommend spreading a layer of soil over the area, sloped at one-half inch per foot, for a distance of 10 feet from the foundation (recall that the drain line from the sump needs to bring the water out at least 10 feet from the basement foundation). Rainwater can enter the basement also through window wells and doors and slabs that slope toward the building. Keep gutters and downspouts in good repair.

A high water table or a building lot at the bottom of a hill are two problems that usually require sump pumps and drainage systems that involve cutting channels along the inside perimeter of the basement walls that carry the water to the sump pit to be pumped out of the drain line periodically. In spite of these measures, however, some parts of the basement

> Many contractors recommend electric floor heating because the drying effects of floor heat will reduce the humidity coming from the slab, which is the largest source of moisture.

> Waterproofing efforts in new construction are often thwarted by homeowners' landscaping efforts along the sides of the foundation, which can change the grading and channel water toward the foundation.

> Drainage for porches was designed so that water would go into the downspout and flow directly into a terra-cotta drain that ran into the soil line and into the sewer or septic tank. Over time, those drain lines can crack and moisture can find its way into the foundation, especially in heavy rainstorms.

Light-gauge steel beams reinforcing a basement ceiling during a renovation have holes for wiring and plumbing prepunched before installation.

Termite barriers in the basement help keep the pests at bay.

Even with perimeter drains channeling the water into the sump, the soil around the basement may be saturated to a point where there is periodic evidence of moisture in the lower portion of the walls, creating efflorescence (water leaches out the salts occurring in the concrete). These areas simply have to be wire brushed and repainted periodically—more for looks than anything else.

It's a good idea not to put flooring directly on the concrete, especially if the water table is already high and can get higher in rainier seasons. Consider installing two-by-two interlocking pieces of the SubFloor Advance System, or the Supra Floor System or DriCore. They have an oriented strand board (OSB) surface layer and a polyethylene base. They also have an R-value that raises the floor temperature a few degrees, and only raises the floor less than an inch, if you are concerned about headroom. Price: $6 per sheet.

may be damper than others and will require extra work controlling moisture before remodeling can occur, or may be difficult to overcome at all.

Once you deal with the moisture problems, or at least get them under control, it will be time to consider the options for remodeling and using your basement. As we've noted so far, we've seen bedrooms and recreation rooms as well as laundry rooms going "down under." Another option is the home office, which was discussed in chapter 4. Obviously, the location of the furnace and ductwork can determine where some of these specialty areas can be placed. Older basements often don't have the right amount of head clearance for remodeling because ductwork and gas and waterlines were hung on the joists, so you have to work around those. In some cases, the floor can be lowered to add more headroom, but that, too, is an expensive proposition.

■ OTHER REMODELING ISSUES

Moisture in the basement is the main issue, but not the only one. In older houses, asbestos, radon, and termite damage are concerns that will need to be addressed before any remodeling work can be undertaken. While all this work should be done by professionals, here's a look at each problem and how it can be handled.

Asbestos

Just because asbestos is there doesn't mean there's a problem. Asbestos may only become harmful when it is damaged and gets into the air. When there is a loose bond, the asbestos can crumble into a powder. It then releases invisible fibers into the air where people can breathe them in. This kind of asbestos is called friable. It usually appears as flakes or chunks of white material that can be easily crumbled by hand pressure. If you see such bare or damaged material, do not disturb it. Some examples of friable asbestos include certain types of insulation found around heating pipes, furnaces, fireproofing, and textured ceilings.

When asbestos is tightly bonded with another material, there is no problem as long as it stays bonded. Examples of bonded material are floor tiles and some roofing and siding shingles. This kind of asbestos is nonfriable and it is not likely to release asbestos fibers. However, cutting, scraping, or sanding this material could release fibers, which could be a health hazard. When materials that contain asbestos are in good shape, they should be left alone. Damaged or worn asbestos material needs special care and handling. If you or your landlord are about to do fix-up work, repairs, or put in a new heating or electrical system, be careful. Asbestos materials must not be disturbed while working.

Asbestos fibers are invisible to the human eye. Because the fibers are so small, light, and fluffy, they can float in the air for a long time. When breathed in, asbestos fibers easily enter the body. Being exposed to asbestos can cause asbestosis, which is scar tissue in the lungs; lung cancer; mesothelioma, which is a cancer of the lining of the lung or abdomen; and gastro-intestinal cancer. The amount of time between first breathing in asbestos and the first signs of disease can vary from 10 to 40 years. The more a person is exposed to asbestos, the more the risk of getting an asbestos-related disease. Cigarette smokers get lung cancer 10 times more often than nonsmokers. Smokers who also breathe in asbestos fibers are up to 92 times more likely to get lung cancer than people who don't smoke and aren't exposed to asbestos.

Radon

Radon is present in elevated levels—higher than the federal limit of four picocuries per liter of air—in nearly 1 of every 15 homes in the country. An exposure level at four picocuries per liter of air is equivalent to having slightly more than 200 chest X rays per year. Radon is a radioactive gas created from the natural decomposition of uranium in soil, rock, and water. It moves up through the ground to the air above and into a house through cracks and holes in the foundation. The gas then remains trapped in the house.

Radon becomes an issue when buyers have children who will be playing in the basement. It is in the basement where the highest concentration of radon gas is found, even though lower levels of radon can be found on upper floors. According to the U.S. Environmental Protection Agency, remediating radon, which is designed to lower the basement reading to two picocuries per liter, costs $700 to $1,400.

Most of the remediation systems are passive, self-venting ones that work by convection—basically a pipe that carries the gas from the basement floor through the roof. If a problem developed, a fan would be added to drive the process. Radon mitigation typically involves sealing cracks and openings in the foundation of the house as well as installing a subslab depressurization system. The typical system is a PVC pipe that is sunk below the concrete floor of the basement and run up through the attic. A fan in the attic sucks the gas through the pipe and out of the house. Sealing the cracks forces the gas to the pipe.

Consider acrylic block for basement windows or interior walls that might take advantage of available natural light. Acrylic blocks are 70 percent lighter than glass. There are also one-piece, acrylic-glass block insert units for interior doors.

Testing typically involves monitoring radon gas levels in the basement for 48 hours. The canister used in the test contains an electrically charged Teflon wafer that reacts to the presence of radon gas. The house has to be closed beginning 12 hours before testing. The wafer is read with a voltage meter at the start of testing. After 48 hours, the wafer is again read with the meter. Oppositely charged ions in the radon gas neutralize the charge on the surface of the wafer, and the resulting reading is the level of gas measured in picocuries per liter of air. After these actions have been taken, another test is done to see whether the level has dropped. A 48-hour test costs $100 to $125. Longer tests—three months is the minimum—run from $125 to $150.

Termites

There are fairly obvious signs of termite infestation that even the layperson can see: pencil-thin mud tubes extending over the inside and outside surfaces of foundation walls, piers, sills, and joists; the presence of winged (swarmer) termites or their shed wings on windowsills and along the edges of floors; and damaged wood hollowed out along the grain and lined with bits of mud or soil. Professional testing is required, however, before the termite problem can be addressed. A nondestructive moisture meter can reveal areas behind the walls that have elevated moisture content. This moisture can be indicative of a plumbing leak, water from a sprinkler system, or precipitation from a roof leak. These all contribute to conditions conducive to infestation by termites, because subterranean termites can utilize the moisture for survival. In these instances, an opening may need to be made in the wall to determine if the moisture is simply from a leak or from an actual termite infestation. The inspector also will use a flashlight, probes, and the power of observation to determine the presence of an infestation. It will require inspecting inside the structure, outside the structure, beneath the structure if there is a pier-and-beam foundation, and in the attic. Termites usually travel inside the timber, forming moist galleries that swell the wood and create a wrinkled surface on the door frame or architrave. Damaged timbers are often paper thin.

A new tool called a Tertramac can detect the movement of termites or other insects inside a wall. Some people also have used trained dogs to detect termites in a structure. During an inspection, areas checked include the subfloor and roof space, interior and exterior, and the site itself (trees and stumps within several feet of the house).

The Gladiator storage system works as well in the basement as in the garage, especially if you don't have a garage (Photo courtesy of the Whirlpool Corp.).

To combat the termites, a complete barrier treatment that could require hundreds of gallons of termiticide solution will be necessary. The water-based solution is injected three to five feet into the ground alongside the foundation, beneath concrete slabs (basement and garage floors, patios, sidewalks, and driveways), and within foundation walls. Pest-control operators use several different termiticides. All are safe and effective when used carefully according to label directions, and will remain effective in the soil for 5 to 10 years. The second option is termite bait, which consists of a palatable and acceptable food material combined with a very slow-acting toxic substance.

■ BASEMENT BATHROOMS

If you are planning a recreation room or a home office, consider a half bath for the basement. The plumbing and soil lines are right there, so it is probably easier putting one in here than on the first or second floors. This is not a do-it-yourself job. You can pick the space and make up a wish list of what you'd like inside it, but you'll need a designer to come up with a plan that will meet your expectations and building code, and a contractor capable of following the plans and the rules.

Pipes are channeled between the joists in the basement ceiling. It makes remodeling easier.

Radiant floor heating systems work well in basements, especially if moisture resistant subflooring is used.

Many homeowners prefer dropped ceilings to drywall in their basements. Dropped ceilings can lower ceiling height if they are not installed properly. Drywall guarantees more height and looks better. Make sure you provide access to plumbing and electrical wiring in that ceiling.

Before you insulate the basement walls, air seal them. You want to keep out colder air that comes in through gaps where foundation meets the floor joists. The least expensive way is to take a white kitchen garbage bag and fill it with unfaced insulation, then stuff it into the gap. Use foam insulation to seal around the insulation bag.

Let's start with design. A design fee is compensation to the designer for advice, consultation, ideas, or development of a bath design or space planning. The fee varies, but expect it to be in the $50- to $75-per-hour range. Some designers apply all or part of the fee toward the project's total cost.

To determine the base costs of installing a theoretical powder room in an existing space (four feet by five feet by seven feet), you'll need to include new walls to enclose the space, which adds to the cost substantially, and, considering the location, you'll need to install moisture-resistant greenboard.

For fixtures, you will want a one-piece, white toilet and a vanity with drop-in sink, for example. A fixture's price depends a great deal on options, such as type and quality of the faucet valve, quality of the finish, and warranty length. A pedestal sink would be cheaper, and charming, but that leaves storage issues with towels and other supplies. Factor in, too, a medicine cabinet with sconce-style lights on each side; an

■ Fast Facts on Building Code Issues for Bathrooms

A clear opening for the door should be at least 32 inches, meaning a minimum door width of 2 feet, 10 inches. The door should not interfere with the safe use of the fixtures or cabinets.

There should be a minimum floor-to-ceiling height of 80 inches.

There should be a clear floor space of at least 30 inches from the front edge of all fixtures to any opposite fixture, wall, or obstacle. The distance from the middle of the sink to the nearest side wall should be 20 inches. The distance from the centerline of the toilet to any other fixture or wall should be at least 18 inches. Flooring should be slip resistant.

The lavatory height may vary between 32 and 43 inches, depending on the users. The countertops should have clipped or rounded corners. There should be adequate, accessible storage for toiletries, bath linens, grooming, and general bathroom supplies at point of use.

Place a mirror above or near the lavatory, at a height that takes users' eye level into consideration.

The toilet-paper holder should be 8 to 12 inches in front of the edge of the toilet bowl, centered at 26 inches above the floor.

exhaust fan, light, and heater; a chrome towel bar; a glass holder; a soap fixture; and a toilet-paper holder.

Standard-grade tile will cost $4 a square foot. There will be a six-panel interior door, two feet by six feet, eight inches. Ceiling and walls will be painted. The decorating, you likely can handle yourself. Have the contractor prime the walls and ceiling, and you can do the finish paint work.

Because the plumbing is easy because of location, the price range for the job is about $6,500 to $8,200.

Glass block windows let light in to basement areas without allowing in cold air or burglars.

A game room in a basement includes a card table and a slot machine. The walkout through French doors leads to a pool.

■ STORING FOOD AND WINE

As consumption grows, more Americans are becoming interested in acquiring and storing fine wines. Storage can be as simple as a cabinet underneath the kitchen counter or as complicated as a temperature- and humidity-controlled basement room. A simple 40-bottle wine cooler runs about $225. A top-of-the-line wine cellar can cost thousands. Still, there are storage systems for just about every budget, and even some that the weekend do-it-yourselfer can handle with the right plans.

A wine cellar's cost depends on the number of bottles you want to store. On the low end, the storage cost averages about $4 per bottle, an increase of $2.50 over the past five years. On the higher end, per-bottle storage costs can be significant, depending on how elaborate your setup is. Racks can be configured for single-bottle storage, double-depth bottle storage, magnums (1.5 liters or twice the capacity of a bottle), and crates, to name a few options.

Many rooms within wine cellars are made of cedar or redwood, which helps keep them dark and damp. Floors can be made of anything, though you need to give materials some consideration. For instance, terra-cotta or tile can be pleasant to look at, but dropping a wine bottle on them can be a shattering experience. Size and location of wine-storage areas may differ, but the contents of the bottles determine how they function.

Wine is properly stored in an environment in which the temperature is 53 to 57 degrees and the humidity ranges between 65 and 70 percent. If a bottle of wine is allowed to get warmer than that, even just for a short time, the aging process is accelerated and, eventually, the liquid turns to vinegar. Keeping the humidity at a constant 65 percent keeps the corks moist. If the corks dry out and shrivel up, air may get into the bottle and spoil the wine.

Have enough room for a prebuilt wine cellar? The GE Monogram Walk-In Wine Vault combines advanced cooling technology, an electronic inventory-management system, insulation, racking, and lighting. It provides storage for more than 1,000 bottles on premium-quality, moisture-resistant redwood racks. Racks are arranged for single-, double-, and triple-bottle storage, while also accommodating magnum bottles and crates. A liquid-based, digital thermostat system offers precise control over temperature, allowing adjustment between 50 and 70 degrees Farenheit, while maintaining ideal humidity conditions. The stainless steel walls and door have high-density foam (R-33 value) that helps ensure temperature and energy-efficient performance. The vault also comes with a system called the Electronic Sommelier, which uses a touch screen monitor and printer. The system has a bar code labeling system and menus that let the user classify each bottle and manage hold time and drink time for each type of wine. Price: $35,000.

GE's Monogram Walk-in Wine Cellar can fit easily into any basement space. Price: $35,000 (Photo courtesy of GE).

Wine bottles, and storage areas, are dark because ultraviolet light can cause wine to deteriorate. Bottles should be tilted so that moisture is kept at the cork. Control systems are designed to create a proper environment for storing wine. If the space is too cold, a control system will warm the area to a proper temperature. If it is too dry, it will add the right amount of moisture.

When REALTOR®/developer Mark Wade produced a show house for the 1999 Remodelers Show, he decided the ideal location for the wine cellar was a cavernous space next to the kitchen, which was in the basement.

"Most buyers reject a basement kitchen as being too dark, but the one we built has a lot of natural light, thanks to the two full windows in the back that looked onto the courtyard," Mark said. "The cellar floor was dirt, so we had to dig down 12 inches to get the right amount of headroom." To get food to the first-floor dining room, Mark installed a dumbwaiter that could support up to 75 pounds.

■ OTHER STORAGE OPTIONS

There are as many ideas for dry basement space as there are homeowners, but the simplest use is for storing extra stuff. No matter how dry the space is, be sure to keep the storage racks away from the walls and off the floors, because that no dry basement is dry all the time, as builder Jim McAleer observes.

Alen didn't need immediate expansion space, but wanted to make absolutely certain that if he ever came up with a need for such a place, the basement would be ready. With that in mind, he hired a company to install a drainage system around the perimeter of his basement.

"The guy first said he was going to use a jackhammer to cut the concrete for the drains, but decided to use a wet saw," Alen said. "In both cases, the workman should have wet down the area to reduce the amount of dust kicked up by the work. He didn't. When the furnace came on, it sucked up the dust floating in the basement air. The furnace blower fan carried the dust to every room in the house."

Alen continues, "It has been three years, and I'm still finding dust."

The basement is a perfect place for an extra bathroom. Learn how much it costs today and check out the best products available at at www.remodelingonthemoney.com

Will It Wash?

11

In the 19th century, clothes were washed in tubs with water heated over open fires and soap made from a combination of lye and ashes. Garments were scrubbed on a board, wrung by hand, rinsed, and hung to dry. Wringer washers arrived before World War I, automatic machines in 1937, dryers in 1949 (although they didn't come into wide use until the 1970s).

This Maytag Neptune washer and dryer fits easily in the home office (Photo courtesy of Maytag Corp.).

Washing clothes in a stream and hanging them in trees to dry might have been enough for our ancestors, but it certainly doesn't fit our lifestyle. Surveys by builders have identified separate laundry rooms as "must-haves" for buyers of average-size houses (2,300 to 2,400 square feet) and upscale houses (4,000 square feet and up). Today, about 75 percent of homes in the country now have a separate laundry room, compared with less than 50 percent in 1975.

Wringer washers involved pumping a foot pedal, which started the motor. The wet clothes were put through the wringer, and a popular expression was born.

Automatic dryers extract moisture from wet clothing by heating and spinning.

■ WHERE TO PUT THE LAUNDRY ROOM

Depending on where they are placed and whether they have more than one purpose, laundry rooms can be as large as 400 square feet—about the size of a starter condo unit in the city—so the question of where to put that laundry room does not have such a clear-cut answer. Recent surveys show that 26 percent of respondents wanted the laundry room near the bedrooms, 26 percent near the kitchen, 23 percent in the basement, and 10 percent in the garage. Homes in a lot of regions, such as Florida, Texas, and areas right on the coasts, don't usually come with basements, so the other locations have to suffice.

Martin and Eleanor recently bought a new washer and dryer that fit perfectly in a narrow hallway leading from the kitchen to a powder room. The couple has a perfectly fine basement with a TV room, playroom, and plenty of storage, but decided that the hallway, which also leads to the garage and the basement, was a preferable choice.

"The plumbing and venting already was there, as was the gas hookup for the dryer," Eleanor said. "We all live on the first floor, that's where the laundry is generated and returned, so even if there is more room in the basement for a washer and dryer, having it there is really inconvenient. And say young Marty comes home muddy from soccer? Would I rather have the washer and dryer near the bathroom where he could just change and toss his uniform and socks out the door to me, or let him track dirt through the house to the basement?"

For Liz and Mike, the basement is their only laundry room option because the floor plan is tight on the first floor, and the second floor is a loft overlooking the family room. What they decided to do, however, was enlarge the basement laundry room by "permanently lending" Mike's pool table, which shared the laundry area, to a relative and

A stacked washer and dryer fits easily in tight spaces.

creating play space for the twin girls and their toddler brother in the spot vacated by the table. That way, the sorting, washing, drying, and folding of an incalculable number of soiled clothing every day can be accomplished with considerable peace of mind.

There have been studies of residential real estate transactions over the past few years that show having a laundry room in the basement can detract from a house's sales price, yet owners of existing houses often have no choice but to put the laundry room in the basement: Apart from the needed space, it often is the place most likely to have ready access to hot water and drainage, and somewhere unobtrusive to vent the dryer.

According to the manufacturers, a load of clothes takes more than two hours from start to finish, including collecting them, transporting them, sorting them, washing them, drying them, returning them to bedrooms, and putting them away. Considering that the typical American family does 8 to 10 loads of wash a week, having the washer and dryer close to where the clothing is dropped off and picked up takes on greater significance.

Whirlpool focuses on laundry as a family occupation, including plenty of storage cabinets (Photo courtesy of Whirlpool Corp.).

"Most older houses either have the laundry room in the basement or on the first floor," says John, a real estate broker. "The first-floor laundry rooms were the result of renovations in the 1970s and 1980s that brought them up from the basement. Some of these smaller older houses had shed rooms or mud rooms off the kitchen that provided ideal spots for laundries. Still, if they had the room, most people would prefer a laundry room on the second floor. That's the ultimate goal of buyers of these houses. And now that stackable washers are standard size, it is a goal that is achievable."

The very fact that both Mike and Liz do the laundry and, from what both say, do it well, puts them at odds with the opinions of most American spouses, at least according to a General Electric consumer survey.

When Maytag Corp. test-marketed its Neptune washer in Bern, Iowa, a few years back, it found that the average Bern family (two adults and two children) did 11 loads a week.

■ Fast Facts on "Laundry Literacy"

Twenty-five percent of women claim their spouses have ruined clothing because of a lack of knowledge about washing techniques and equipment.

Women are more likely than men to follow preventive and maintenance procedures, including closing zippers and hooks while sorting clothes, turning down cuffs, separating delicates, and reading care labels.

Forty-three percent of women and 47 percent of men still don't know when to use a powder or liquid detergent.

Ten percent of men have never done wash.

Seventy-two percent of Americans believe that doing the laundry should be a shared chore.

Twenty-three percent of women claim their partners have never ruined clothing, simply because they have never participated in doing laundry.

Maytag model MAV9750 has a finger faucet under the rim that you can use to wash laundry soap off your hands. It also has a "remind chime" that tells you when the wash is done, which is easier than putting your ear to the floor if the washer and dryer are in the basement.

Need to wash your delicates in something that you can keep clean? Whirlpool's Sink Spa system has three microjets that direct the swirling action of the water in a deep-basin sink, meaning that you also can do small loads. The jets operate on a one-horsepower pump. There's a 10-minute timer and a washboard etched on the inside front of the sink for scrubbing. Price: $599.

Barbara traveled up and down the basement stairs of her semidetached house several times a week to do the laundry, but when she and husband Joe bought a detached house a few blocks away, Barbara decided that she wanted to put the laundry room on the second floor—the location of all the bedrooms—thinking correctly that it would save her a lot of work. The ideal location was a large half bath that the family, which was getting smaller as the three children were moving out, no longer used.

One plumber she contacted declined the job, saying that he was concerned about water overflowing from the washer into the room below. Another plumber was not so reticent, and the washer and dryer have been doing their job without incident for the past 10 years.

If you want a second-floor laundry room for the sake of convenience, there are some things you need to consider beforehand. An area 6 feet wide by 3 feet deep would accommodate a standard-size washer and dryer, a utility tub, and maybe a hamper. A stackable washer/dryer unit could save space horizontally. A 7½- or 8-foot ceiling would provide more than enough height for a couple of shelves to hold supplies and detergent above the washer and dryer. But is that enough room to meet your needs? Not necessarily. You might want additional space for sorting dirty laundry and folding clean clothes, and maybe even for an ironing board.

Try to place the laundry room near existing plumbing and wiring, and preferably in the rear of the house, so that the vent is unobtrusive. Building codes require flexible ductwork for the dryer vent and shut-off valves for the water. If the room is on the other side of the master bath, you'll need to insulate to deaden the sound. You may need to bring in a structural engineer to see whether your floor joists can withstand a washer's vibration. If not, the floor will need reinforcing.

You'll need 6 inches of clearance behind the dryer for the venting duct and gas connections (if you're using gas). Most dryers are 30 to 32 inches deep. Building codes also require that the washer sit in an overflow pan to prevent water from pouring onto the floor and into the ceiling below.

Doors can be solid or louvered, but with solid ones you will need a mechanical way (a vent with

Miele's Professional series washer and dryer cost $35,000 and readout panel is in four languages (Photo courtesy of Miele).

Maytag's Neptune Drying Center looks like something that might fit in that second-floor laundry room, especially if there is room on top, because it occupies the floor space of a normal dryer. The drying center pairs a Neptune tumble dryer with an upper drying cabinet designed to reduce shrinkage, speed up the drying process, control wrinkles, eliminate odors, and refresh clothes. As many as 13 items can be hung in the upper cabinet, which eliminates the need for a separate rack for hanging clothes. The dryer can handle bulky bedspreads and rugs, too. Price: $1,200.

Maytag's cordless iron comes in two models, one with a titanium sole plate and electronic temperature controls, the other with a stainless steel sole plate and mechanical dial controls. Although the iron needs an electric outlet for charging, it doesn't need one for ironing, enhancing its versatility. It also shuts off after 10 minutes if left unattended. The iron has a snap-off water tank for easier filling; with the tank removed, it easily reaches into small, tight spaces such as shirt cuffs. Price: $129 to $149, depending on the model.

a fan) to bring enough air into the space for proper combustion for a gas dryer. This is not an issue with an electric dryer. There should be three feet of clearance for the door so the washer and dryer can be moved in and out of the laundry room easily.

An ironing board folds into a drawer (Photo courtesy of KitchenAid).

Plan for plenty of lighting. And there should be ground fault circuit interrupter (GFCI) outlets that will shut off automatically if they come into contact with moisture. You may want to replace existing drywall with moisture-resistant greenboard, but it isn't necessary.

> Whirlpool's ImPress Ironing Station can be installed in a cabinet or on the wall. The ironing board, which swivels 360 degrees, is height-adjustable and stores with minimum effort. The unit has a place to store the iron as it cools, along with ironing accessories. It also has its own work light and electrical receptacle. Price: $599.

> Some machines are billed as having washing and drying cycles. One washer tub extracts 24 percent more water from clothes than the industry standard, which means less drying time. Less time in the dryer lengthens the life of your clothes because heat damages them.

■ NEW TRENDS

Although Mike and Liz's laundry room is in the wrong location according to today's trend watchers, the fact that the space is doing double duty as a play area means that they are creating their own, much less pricey version of the Whirlpool Laundry Studio, which debuted a few years back. The idea behind the concept was to have a place where the kids could gather round as the wash was being done—a combined workroom/ playroom that, when included in a new house, would add about $30,000 to the price—leading to the comment at the beginning of this chapter.

The whole-room approach is designed to take advantage of the growth in the size of laundry rooms, according to Whirlpool spokeswoman Audrey Reed-Granger. They're one-third to one-half larger now than they used to be, because they've been either built bigger or expanded during a home renovation.

"The trend is toward treating a laundry room as if it were a suite," Audrey says. "More of them are appearing on the first and second floors, and because of the new location, they're becoming showplaces. They are being connected to the interior design of the house and are being shown off with everything else."

That's why Whirlpool has introduced a stain- and scratch-resistant work surface ($199) for folding and sorting laundry that can be fitted around its Duet washers ($600 to $1,400) and dryers ($759 to $929).

"Every room of the house has become an individual living experience," Audrey says. "The laundry room is a big part of that."

Whirlpool's KitchenAid division has taken another tack. Instead of creating a

In 1996, a house designed for women featured a laundry room in an out-of-the-way spot between the kitchen and garage, and had a chute from the upstairs to save today's career woman from collecting laundry from every room in her home. The laundry room is all-inclusive, with an iron and ironing board, a closet, and compartmentalized bins for laundry baskets. Some fire officials, however, don't like chutes, believing that they may spread fire.

KitchenAid pushes the multipurpose laundry room, which includes enough room for an exercise bike (Photo courtesy of KitchenAid).

Miele's washers have honeycomb drums with tiny holes so laundry won't get caught and wear out (Photo courtesy of Miele).

room for the laundry, it is selling the Pro-Line Fabric Care System—a paired stainless steel washer and dryer ($7,000) designed to fit into master suites, kitchens, or other visible areas of the home. The appliance maker says that trends show consumers are turning their laundry areas into more of a sanctuary by incorporating custom cabinetry and storage options along with items like televisions,

How many laundry rooms does one house need? The 10,000-plus-square-foot 2006 New American Home at the International Builders Show in Orlando, Florida, featured six—including one in the guest-room suite.

GE's Profile Harmony Clothes Care front-loading laundry pair features an energy- and water-saving Hydro-Motion wash system, which rotates in two directions; an internal water heater that increases water temperature to improve wash performance of particularly tough stains on loads like white cottons; and a system that can inspect and treat 80 stains. Washers range from $999 to $1,049, dryers from $849 to $949. While some manufacturers emphasize style, others focus on noise reduction. Bosch Appliance's Nexxt line of washers and dryers have a capacity to 3.81 cubic feet, higher speeds, and what the company says is the lowest silence rating among front-end washers.

Miele spent considerable effort coming up with a way of doing laundry that reduces the wear and tear on clothing. The Touchtronic line of residential washers costs $1,700 to $2,100, and dryers run $1,400 to $1,800. Both have a honeycomb drum, introduced in 2005, which features smaller holes so clothes have less of a chance to get caught and tear.

GE has taken a small step back from touch-screen technology—not abandoning it but—giving consumers the option of using traditional dials to program in wash cycles to make operating the washers easy and understandable for everyone.

coffeemakers, and CD players. Laundry areas are evolving beyond the bare bones of just a washer and dryer to a more luxurious space to spend time in.

While it isn't new, Whirlpool's Personal Valet continues to catch on because it does offer the chance to have a dry-cleaning unit in one's house. The Valet smooths wrinkles and removes odors from up to three garments at a time in 30 minutes. The Valet uses Presiva, a water-based formula that, when heat activated, revitalizes clothes. The company has come out with a portable version for $219.

The company also is finding success marketing its commercial line of washers and dryers to high-end residential customers (those able to afford staff to do their laundry, because the control-panel language options include English, Spanish, German, and Italian). The price tag for the pair is $35,000. There is a commercial rotary iron for $9,900; the residential version costs $2,000.

If you have minimal space but want to do the laundry somewhere other than the dingy basement, take a look at stackables, both compact and full size. That's what Jim and Trish chose to do 11 years ago when they bought a house and decided to live on the top two floors and rent out the first floor. The basement had a dirt floor and was only accessible from the outside, and rather than buy two sets of washers and dryers, they placed a stackable in a closet on the first floor near the tenants but at the end of the stairs to their part of the house. Tenants have changed, and the couple has added three children, and still the laundry arrangement is workable. They are, however, on their second stackable.

■ Fast Facts on Stackable Washer/Dryers

GE's Spacemaker is a 24-inch stackable washer with an enlarged 2.7-cubic-foot capacity, increasing the amount of clothes you can wash, and thus reducing the number of loads. The advantage: It takes up much less space than separate appliances. A built-in fluorescent light shines down from the stack rack to illuminate the wash tub. The washer has a bifold lid that lifts up and slides back; an electronic touch pad for programming; a load-sensing monitor that keeps the water at proper levels; a stainless steel tub; high-speed spin that eliminates more water and speeds drying time; and 10 cycle options. Price: $500 (washer alone). Adding a dryer boosts the price to $1,000.

The 27-inch-wide Frigidaire Galley has a full-size, front-loading washer. The dryer has a moisture sensor, which can tell when clothes are dry. Controls for both the washer and the dryer are mounted in the center of the unit. It needs a 220-volt power supply and standard venting. Price: $1,000 for both.

Whirlpool's big-selling Duet washer and dryer are stackable, but stacking them puts the dryer controls at the top of the six feet of laundry center you'll create (the cost is almost $2,300 for the pair). A better stackable option from Whirlpool is the 27 3/8-inch-wide Thin Twin with a 2.5-cubic-foot wash basket, and six cycles for each, which only requires a 15 or 20 amp circuit. Price: $1,100 for the unit.

LG Industries has the SenseClean 75, a combination washer and dryer in which you put clothes to wash, then pick them up when they are dry (about 80 minutes later). The front-loading SenseClean can easily fit in an apartment closet. Best of all, it is vent-less. The humidity from the drying process condenses and goes out the same drain as the dirty washer water. The SenseClean has a direct-drive system—without belts and pulleys—that makes it both quiet and energy efficient. Price: $1,499.

The Kenmore 24-inch stackable with electric dryer has a self-cleaning lint filter, the washer basket is 1.5 cubic feet, and the dryer has a 3.4-cubic-foot interior. The wash motion is a dual-action agitator. It isn't ENERGY STAR compliant, but is reasonably priced and offers full-size washing and drying in a small package. Price: $850.

■ WASHERS

There has been a lot of discussion about the merits of vertical axis and horizontal-axis washers and energy savings. Traditionally, American-made washers have been top-loading, vertical-axis machines with agitators in the

Frigidaire designed a laundry room for men shown at the 2006 Kitchen & Bath Show in Chicago. Featured along with the Affinity washer ($799) and dryer ($599), were a giant flat-screen TV and an electronic streaming scoreboard.

LG Electronics sells a washer that incorporates steam technology to help reduce wrinkles ($1,499 to $1,599) and the Tromm convertible laundry system, which enables you to place the control panel at either the top or the bottom of the dryer unit ($1,199 to $1,299 for the washer, $999 to $1,099 for the dryer). Acknowledging growing diversity in the laundry-gear market, the control panel has a multilingual option that includes English, French, and Spanish.

middle of the tubs. In Europe, where energy is costly, horizontal-axis washers are the rule. In a horizontal-axis, front-loading washer, the tub is tilted slightly forward and tumbles like a dryer. Less water is used per load, and because of that, drying time is also reduced, saving both water and electricity.

In 1997, the U.S. Bureau of Reclamation, in its never-ending search for ways to reduce water consumption, was trying to determine how much water a horizontal-access machine would save compared with vertical-axis one. Maytag was just introducing its Neptune horizontal-axis

washer to the U.S. market, so the Environmental Protection Agency's ENERGY STAR Residential Technology Program talked Maytag into providing 104 Neptune washers to Bern, Iowa, for the test. An ENERGY STAR rating on an appliance is a government-backed guarantee that any product with the symbol will use 30

Whirlpool stacked washer and dryer fits in a former half bath (Photo courtesy of Whirlpool Corp.).

percent less energy each year than the national standard, but the EPA will not award such a designation without lengthy testing under actual conditions.

Because the new Maytag washers retail at $999 to $1,519, depending on the model, it was not an inexpensive proposition. In return, the residents had to agree to submit to scientific scrutiny and do laundry when the government told them to. Because vertical-axis machines use about 38 gallons of water to wash 12 pounds of

Sears has begun offering washers and dryers in Pacific Blue, Champagne, and Sedona—colors the surveys found were preferred by most buyers. The washers and dryers retail for close to $1,000 each. Despite the emphasis on color, Sears acknowledged that "cleanability" was more important than anything else to consumers. The new washers are energy efficient and can handle 23 bath towels, if you actually own that many.

Go shopping for the most efficient washers at www.remodelingonthemoney.com

Miele's stacked washer and dryer with a clothespress (Photo courtesy of Miele).

clothes—just about what it takes to quench a cow's thirst on a hot day—they readily agreed.

Two water meters were installed on each washer in the project: one to measure hot water consumption; the other for cold. The temperatures of the hot and cold water were carefully measured when the meters were installed, then measured again after the horizontal-access washers were put in. Each participant was given a scale for weighing wash loads in a standard laundry basket, which also was supplied. Everyone received a standard detergent cup to measure what they used per load and record it.

On average, the horizontal-axis washer used 62.2 percent of the water used by the vertical-axis washer, and this yielded total water savings of 37.8 percent. Moreover, the average horizontal-axis washer consumed 42.4 percent of the energy used by a typical vertical-axis washer in the study, resulting in energy savings of 57.6 percent. Put more

If you are planning to introduce a horizontal-axis washer to an upper-floor laundry room, plumbers suggest having a structural engineer look at the joists. Higher-speed spinning can increase machine vibration, and the floor joists of older houses can weaken over time.

succinctly, a vertical-axis washer used 8 gallons of hot water and 30 gallons of cold to wash a 12-pound load of clothes. A horizontal-axis machine used 4.4 gallons of hot water and 15.3 gallons of cold.

If your washing machine is more than 10 years old, and you can afford a new one, it's time to think about replacing it. Today's models not only save water and energy, they're designed to keep you from making the kind of mistakes that turn your brilliant whites into dull pinks.

A sewing machine fits easily on a pullout platform (Photo courtesy of KitchenAid).

■ Fast Facts on Washers

The choice is between front-loading and top-loading models. In a top-loading machine, an agitator moves the laundry in water and detergent to get it clean; after the wash cycle, the clothes are spun at a high speed to remove detergent and water. The washer refills, the agitator moves the items through the water to remove remaining detergent, and then they're spun again. A regular wash cycle uses about 45 gallons of water.

A first-floor laundry room off the kitchen.

Higher-efficiency front loaders are built on a horizontal access and fill to just below the door opening, which reduces the water used to about 25 gallons. Clothes move with a tumbling action through the water, causing less wear and tear on the fabrics and seams. Front loaders can cost more, but the payback in savings is coming more quickly as energy prices climb.

What do a washer's cycle options really offer, and do you need them? Computerization has enabled manufacturers to tune wash cycles very finely, but most selections are just slight variations on the basics: regular, permanent press, prewash/soak (for tough stains); heavy, and gentle/delicate. Permanent press and regular cycles are virtually the same, for example, but permanent press cools items before the spinning starts to prevent wrinkling. A gentle cycle agitates and spins items more slowly to protect delicate fabrics. A heavy cycle offers a longer wash time and more rinses.

Today's washers come with more water temperature options, too, but again you should look for the basics. Most washers offer hot, warm, and cold water wash cycles and cold rinse cycles. A hot water wash cleans whites and heavily soiled items better, but uses more energy than warm and cold wash cycles do. The temperature of the hot and warm washes depends on what's supplied by your water heater. To change warm water temperature, you have to change the mix of hot and cold water at the faucet.

What it will cost: $300 to $1,500, though you can pay more for added speed and cycle combos, larger capacity, and a wider variety of water temperatures and levels. Spend wisely: Don't buy more washer than you need.

Before buying, check the Energy Guide label, which shows the estimated annual energy consumption in kilowatt-hours per year and the estimated annual operating cost. A washer bearing the ENERGY STAR label meets strict efficiency guidelines set by the U.S. Environmental Protection Agency and Department of Energy.

Full loads save water and energy, so be sure to match water level, temperature, and the amount of detergent to the load's size. Don't jam clothes into the washer too tightly; it'll wear out faster. After each load, turn the water off at the faucets to relieve pressure on the hoses. If the washer has a lint filter, clean it frequently.

■ DRYERS

■ Fast Facts on Dryers

The most energy-friendly way to dry laundry is on a clothesline, but the easiest way is with an electric or gas dryer. Dryers don't vary much in energy consumption from model to model, but there are other factors to consider before you buy one, such as the following:

A dryer's efficiency is measured by something known as the "energy factor," which is similar to the miles-per-gallon rating of a car. Energy factor is measured in pounds of clothing per kilowatt-hour of electricity. So the more clothes you can dry per kilowatt-hour, the cheaper your dryer will be to run. The minimum energy factor for a standard-capacity electric dryer is 3.01. For gas dryers, the minimum is 2.67, based on a natural-gas equivalent of the same kilowatt-hour measurement used for an electric dryer.

Drum capacity for a full-size dryer is 5 to 7 cubic feet, and you'll want to coordinate it with the capacity of your washer. For example, a washer with a 3.5-cubic-foot capacity requires 7 cubic feet of dryer capacity.

All dryers use heat to extract moisture from clothes as they tumble—and the amount of work the dryer has to do depends, of course, on the amount of water remaining in the clothes when they come out of the washer. Newer dryer models aim to minimize running time. The best models have moisture sensors in the drum that can save you up to 15 percent of drying time, but most models estimate dryness by sensing the temperature of the exhaust air.

Look for a dryer with a cycle that includes a cool-down period, sometimes known as a permanent-press cycle. In the last few minutes of this cycle, cool air rather than heated air is blown through the tumbling clothes to complete the drying process.

Every dryer uses a small electric motor to turn the drum so the clothes can tumble. All have electric fans to spread the heated air evenly. That's where the similarities between gas and electric dryers end.

Electric dryers supply heat through coils that require a 240-volt current to work. The typical outlet is 120 volts, so you might have to call an electrician to make the necessary change. Gas dryers use a burner to create heat; for one of these, you'll need a gas hookup, a safe way to vent the gas, and a 120-volt electric outlet for that blower and fan.

If your laundry room is set up for both gas and electric, consider price. Gas dryers cost $50 more than similar electric models, but in many areas natural gas is less expensive than electricity, so you could recoup the extra costs over the life of the dryer. (The typical dryer lasts about 18 years.)

Standard-capacity electric dryers cost $200 to $1,000; gas, $250 to $1,100. Compact dryers range from $200 to $700. These space-saving units can be stacked on top of companion washers that often work like regular-capacity models, so they need a 240-volt line. There also are combination washers and dryers on the market that do both jobs in a single machine. Smaller-capacity combos start around $700. Standard-size combos range from $1,200 to $1,600.

■ ENERGY-SAVING TIPS

A walk-in closet becomes a laundry room in this city house.

If you cannot afford to replace your current washer and dryer, there are ways to save energy.

If laundry rooms are getting more elaborate, appliances are getting more technologically sophisticated. Manufacturers are producing washers and dryers that take up less room yet can do several loads of laundry in the same amount of time it used to take to do one.

Thanks to the sophisticated high-tech wiring being introduced into a growing number of new houses, washer and dryer operations can be monitored from TV screens in any part of the house. This technology also is allowing the homeowner to keep an eye on the health of these appliances. Washers and dryers—and kitchen appliances, for that matter—can tell a homeowner when maintenance is due or when it's time to be replaced.

The appliance, that is, not the consumer.

■ Fast Facts on Saving Energy

For the washer, use lower temperature settings to achieve the same cleaning results. Use warm or cold water for wash cycles (hot water for grease stains) and cold water for all rinse cycles. Use recommended amounts of cold water detergents. Wash full loads. If washing a smaller load, use the appropriate water-level setting. Insulate hot water pipes and locate the washer close to the water heater.

For the dryer, separate clothes and dry similar types together (lightweight loads and heavy loads) to prevent overdrying and excessive energy use. Dry full loads when possible, but be careful not to overfill the dryer; clothes will take longer to dry without space to tumble. Don't overdry clothes. If the machine has a moisture sensor, use it.

Dry two or more loads in a row, taking advantage of residual heat in the dryer. Clean the lint filter after every load to improve air circulation. Check the outside dryer vent for lint clogs or possible air filtration. Locate the dryer in a heated space. Dry clothes for free on an outside clothesline or inside drying rack.

Decking and Paving
the Outdoors

12

Alex and Beth's deck was in the way of the two-story addition that would double the size of their house—right where the new kitchen and family room were to take shape. So contractor Jay Cipriani had his carpentry crew disassemble the deck piece by piece, numbering each piece after photographing how the deck looked, and then storing the pieces of the deck for the next few months until the addition was completed.

Then, in reverse order, the deck was reassembled so that the new French doors from the family room would open seamlessly onto the deck and the couple's

Decking is fitted between the posts before the railing is added.

two sons, Ben and Cole, would have easy access to the weatherproof toys that tend to overflow to the out of doors. Of course, Jay's crew had to dig new footings for the deck and replace some of the worn boards and railings that didn't survive deconstruction, but, unless you really looked closely, you couldn't tell the difference.

"We really liked the old deck," Beth says, "and didn't want to change it. In addition, starting a new deck from scratch would have cost a lot more than reconstructing the existing one, and when you

157

Design the deck as something other than a rectangle. Consider using laminated safety glass instead of pickets for the railing so the view is not blocked.

A lot of builders make decks optional, suggesting to buyers that they could probably find someone to build it cheaper, and put a couple of boards in front of the French doors where the deck will be.

are building a major addition, you need to look for ways to save money where you can."

David and Elizabeth added a deck to their house, but did it the hard way. They bought a house for $1 and had it moved in two sections 25 miles to a lot they owned next to David's workshop. Once the house was in place, David built a 900-square-foot deck made of mahogany and cedar about three-quarters of the way around the building. While cedar is not an unusual deck material, mahogany is used by only the well-to-do or by woodworkers such as David, who know where to get great quantities of such exotic lumber at reasonable prices and who collect discarded wood from lumber mills as a sideline. Western red cedar runs anywhere from $1.20 to $2.00 a linear foot; mahogany decking runs $3.00 to $6.00 a linear foot, depending on width and quality.

What was really unusual, however, was the railing. The former site of the house was surrounded by a fence made of Louisiana yellow locust, which David salvaged and milled into the railings for the deck. The lumber is rare, and David and Elizabeth, who are environmentalists at heart, never once considered throwing it in a dumpster.

Composite decking is used on this play area near a swimming pool. Composite decking is virtually maintenance free.

TenduraPlank is a composite lumber that has been on the market for three years and is used on porches and decks. It is fungus and termite resistant and is made to expand and contract less than lumber. The tongue-and-groove decking is available in two widths, 3 1/8 inches and 5 1/4 inches.

■ DECKS

As the decades have passed, more new homes have come with features conducive to outdoor activities. In recent years, 46 percent of new homes came with patios, compared with 37 percent 30 years ago; 53 percent came with porches, compared with 42 percent; and 37 percent came with decks, compared with

Watch a deck rise from concept to outdoor entertainment center at www.remodelingonthemoney.com

A drill attachment is used to put screws in decking to hold it to the frame.

27 percent 30 years earlier. Decks are especially popular in the northeastern United States—they are featured in 43 percent of new homes, compared to 25 percent in the mid-1970s.

Before 1970, decks were rare. Then, as outdoor entertaining grew popular and brick and concrete patios became more expensive, the wooden deck emerged. At first, the majority of decks were made of cedar or redwood, both of which stand up well to moisture. When those woods started rising in price, homeowners began turning to pressure-treated lumber such as Southern pine treated with chromated copper arsenate (CCA), a chemical mixture consisting of three pesticidal compounds—arsenic, chromium, and copper—to keep the termites and other wood-loving pests away. The lumber came with a 40-year guarantee.

Lumber treated with CCA, which has been used in deck construction for many years, is no longer being sold for residential use, and alternative lumber products treated with alkaline copper quaternary (ACQ) or copper azole (CA) are now on the market, sold under a variety of names (ACQ Preserve and NatureWood, among them).

There are important issues surrounding the new products, too, and you need to be informed before you buy pressure-treated lumber or sign a contract for deck construction or repair. Some new products, for instance, are treated with sodium borate (sold as Advanced Guard or Dura-Bora). Unlike ACQ and CA, lumber treated with borates should not come into contact with moisture, and so cannot be used outdoors in decks or as sill plates in home construction. In addition, unlike ACQ and CA, borates do not bond with wood all that well.

For the greatest financial return, many builders and real estate agents suggest that the deck be designed as an extension of the living space, not an appendage to the house.

Most people tend to build their decks too small for furniture and for function. Add a couple more feet than you think you'll need.

Each contractor should provide a detailed estimate of the project, including a description of the materials, how they will be used, how much the project will cost, and about how long it will take. The contractor handles all permit and inspection requirements and builds the cost of them into the price. Many provide the required scale drawings once the contract has been signed.

> The average sizes of decks for spec and custom houses are calculated to be 252 and 407 square feet, respectively.

The new treated-lumber varieties cost about 10 percent more than the old lumber—some say 20 percent more depending on region—but the price will likely drop as more ACQ products reach the market. And fortunately, this lumber resembles CCA-treated lumber in color, so it can be used to replace boards in older decks. Many environmental advocates, however, have suggested that homeowners wishing to replace CCA-treated decking use composite lumber such as Trex rather than the new treated lumber, on the off chance that ACQ and CA are found to be problematic over the long term.

Composite decking now accounts for 5 percent of the $3.5 billion annual decking market, and costs about 50 percent more on average than pressure-treated lumber. There are more than 40 material options for decks, both natural and man made. All these alternatives are for decking only. They aren't strong enough for posts or joists, which remain the job of pressure-treated lumber.

Trex, a wood-and-plastic composite, is made primarily from equal parts reclaimed hardwood sawdust and reclaimed and recycled polyethylene plastic, such as grocery sacks and stretch film. The plastic is supposed to shield the wood from moisture and insect damage. The wood protects the plastic from UV damage and provides additional stability and traction.

For mold, mildew, and berry and leaf stains, conventional deck washes containing detergent and sodium hypochlorite work well. For rust stains or ground-in dirt and grime, use cleaners containing phosphoric acid that

Pressure-treated decking is used in combination with vinyl railing for this deck.

are available in home and hardware centers. For tougher oil and grease stains, scrub with a detergent containing a degreasing agent as soon as possible after the stain occurs. For grease stains that have set, try a light hand-sanding with fine sandpaper.

Trex also sells a railing system, as does TimberTech, which offers tongue-and-groove decking made from recycled wood and virgin plastic (not recycled plastic bags), as well as standard two-by-six decking and TimberTopper

> There are about 30 million residential decks. More than 6.5 million decks are built in the United States annually, at a total cost of $1.9 to $3 billion.

covers that can be used to refinish a worn deck. CertainTeed's Boardwalk line also includes decking and railing. It is made with EcoTech, which combines polyvinyl chloride and natural wood fibers. Boardwalk and the other composites tend to be slip resistant. Most sealers used to waterproof wooden decks contain

> The five most popular materials used in new homes to build decks are pressure-treated lumber, Western red cedar, concrete, redwood, and plastic.

paraffin, which is wax, as a preservative. If you put too much on the decking, it can get slippery. These composites don't need to be sealed or stained. Louisiana-Pacific's WeatherBest comes in decking and railing. The decking is either solid or hollow; the hollow is lighter and can be used with up to 24-inch on-center joists. The solid decking can be used on up to 16-inch on-center spans. Pricing varies, so it's best to check with local contractors and suppliers. In general, composite tends to cost more than pressure-treated wood, but the price will go down as it captures more of the market.

■ A Deck Building Primer

Whether you're overseeing a contractor's work or have time to do it yourself, here's how building a deck proceeds:

Post holes are dug, with a shovel or post-hole digger, according to the specifications established by the local building department, which will inspect them after they are done. Concrete is then poured for the footings—about 450 to 500 pounds for each hole. Footings can be built on 24 hours after they've been poured. A heavy "ledger board," typically a 2-by-12, is attached to the house with galvanized bolts or 40d nails. Joists will be attached to the ledger board using metal joist hangers.

Posts, either 4 by 4 or 6 by 6, that support the deck are anchored to the footings. The 2-by-10 joists are attached from the ledger board to a crossbeam that has been attached to the posts. Most contractors use metal joist

hangers to attach the joists, but some bolt the crossbeam to the posts so that the weight rests on the bolts.

The flooring and 4-by-4 rail posts are attached. On a wide deck, decking boards of varying lengths are used instead of a single length to avoid having a seam down the middle.

Railings are built in sections by attaching 2-by-2 balusters a few inches apart to 2-by-4 precut cross rails so that the balusters will be on the inside rather than the outside of the deck—they look better that way. The railings are attached to the rail posts, which are notched to accept the railings flush. Then the rail posts are cut to make them even with the railings. The railings are capped, typically with a fairly wide board, often a 5/4 by 6.

Stairs are built. Options such as benches or lattice work are built at this time.

So far, neither CA nor ACQ has environmental concerns attached to it, and ACQ's toxicity is much lower than CCA's. Still, it is recommended that you take the same precautions that you would with CCA-treated lumber: wash your hands after contact, don't cut the lumber in enclosed spaces, and wear gloves and safety goggles while doing so. These new treatments, while considered less harmful to humans than the arsenic in CCA, can cause a different problem: They can corrode metal connectors and fasteners more quickly. That's because they contain a higher level of copper than wood treated with CCA.

A reciprocating saw is used to cut the deck post to size before the vinyl railing is added.

Every municipality has its own requirements for decks and their builders. In some, builders must be licensed; most are required to be insured. Other towns require that a scale drawing of the deck plan be reviewed by the building inspector.

Stainless steel connectors or fasteners cannot be used in combination with hot-dipped galvanized connectors or fasteners. The more zinc on the surface of a hot-dipped galvanized fastener, the better it can limit corrosion. A lot of fastener manufacturers have been increasing the amount of zinc—some up to 50 percent more—to improve product performance. Be aware, however, that galvanized fasteners are rust resistant, not rustproof. Nothing says the fasteners will stay rust free.

There has been some concern about that copper leaching into water supplies during rainstorms, but there has been no data from government agencies addressing that potential (The U.S. Environmental Protection Agency is in the final year of a two-year study on the most effective method of sealing CCA decks to prevent the arsenic from escaping.).

Manufacturers say that hot-dipped galvanized or stainless steel fasteners and fittings are acceptable for use with ACQ-treated wood. Aluminum fasteners and fittings are not. Hot-dipped galvanized and stainless steel fasteners always have been recommended for use in deck construction, but they cost more than the aluminum and electroplated galvanized fittings commonly used, though hot-dipped fasteners tend to be less expensive than stainless steel. Corrosion is a process in which metal deteriorates through a chemical reaction with the environment. Some preservatives can promote the corrosion process by providing more favorable conditions for the conversion of metal into the products of corrosion.

Brick pavers were used for this patio. Patterns are limited and there usually is a lot of cutting involved.

A study found that the new preservatives were twice as corrosive as CCA. The rate of corrosion depends on other things, including salt water or air containing it, pollutants, wood preservatives, the presence of other metals, temperature, and relative humidity.

Some builders and even more do-it-yourselfers have not yet gotten the word about the fastener and fitting problems. Building officials are concerned. One building official reported inspecting three decks that were constructed with ACQ wood and standard (electroplated, not hot-dipped) galvanized hangers and aluminum flashing. He ordered that the fasteners and fittings be changed, which proved costly and time consuming for both the homeowner and contractor.

That's the solution when decks are built legally, but as building officials realize all too well, a big portion of the estimated 30 million residential decks in the United States have been built by do-it-yourselfers and contractors without official sanction. Although home centers no longer carry CCA-treated lumber, they often stock all the fasteners on the same shelf, without any distinction of which should be used with what lumber. It remains the responsibility of builders and do-it-yourselfers, then, to make sure that they are using the right fasteners and fittings for the job.

Among the products acceptable for use with the new lumber are Simpson's ZMAX (G185) hot-dip galvanized or stainless steel fasteners; USP structural connectors/triple zinc G-185 connectors; PrimeSource fastening systems (PrimeGuard Plus coated fasteners); and Osmose Pro-Drive screws, Bostich Thickcoat.

There are several staining options, including clear water repellent without UV protection, which lets the deck gray with cracking, or clear with UV protection, which prevents graying. You should seal every year, no matter which you use. Semitransparent and solid stains with sealers come in a variety of hues and let you go as many as three years without restaining, depending on your climate and the location of the deck. Remember, if you strip a stained deck, you are going to have to restain.

There are plenty of ways to extend the summer into other parts of the year. That means outdoor heaters, which can be placed on patios or decks to take the chill out of the autumn evening air after the mosquitoes quit the scene.

■ Fast Facts on Cleaning Your Deck

Removing accumulated grime and mildew is best done on cooler, cloudy days that allow the deck to stay wetter longer and give the cleaner time to work.

You'll need to know the square footage of the deck, including stairs and railings, to figure out how much cleaner and sealer you need. A gallon of stain or sealer typically covers 150 to 300 square feet of deck. (Commercial deck cleaner typically lists square-foot coverage on the package.)

If screw or nail heads have popped up above the surface of the deck, make sure they're back in place before you start your work to avoid injury and damage to cleaning implements.

Apply cleaner (available at home centers and online) with a paintbrush or a sprayer. Let the cleaner work into the deck surface for about 15 minutes, then remove the residue with a squeeze mop; dirtier decks may require more than one application. Don't scrub, even if dirt and mildew are really imbedded, to avoid gouging the softwood used in most decking.

Allow two or three days of good drying after cleaning before applying a waterproof sealer. Mild weather (55 to 70 degrees) is perfect. If it's too hot and dry, the sealer will dry too quickly and won't permeate the deck surface. If it's too warm and humid, the sealer will take too long to dry, and there is a greater chance that wind, leaves, animals, and rain will disturb the surface, which can result in an uneven coating.

Some experts advise against using power washers on deck surfaces because pressure can damage softwood. But using a power washer saves time. Before you rent one at a home center or rental outlet, ask what you should use. The appropriate washer for this kind of job typically delivers 1,500 to 2,100 pounds of pressure per square inch.

Watch out for the following bad advice: "This cleaner won't harm plants." Even if the manufacturer's label tells you that, cover plants under or near the deck with plastic sheeting, or soak the plants with enough water to neutralize any cleaning solution that spills onto them.

Bleach and water is the cheapest deck cleaner. A 69-cent quart of liquid bleach will be more than enough; use a mixture of three parts water to one part bleach. Deck cleaners available at the home center come in powder and liquid and cost $5 to $15 for 16 to 32 ounces. Stains cost $15 to $25 a gallon. Water-repellant sealers run $15 to $20 a gallon.

Deck sealers can be water repellents or water-repellent preservatives (WRPs). Water repellents are either water based or oil based; the latter use organic solvents such as mineral spirits or turpentine. Whether water or oil based, the products typically are mixed with linseed oil or varnish or paraffin wax, which is why wood on a treated deck can feel like a candle.

WRPs add a mildewcide, an ingredient designed to limit the appearance of mildew, for better performance. They take a short time to apply—maybe only an hour—and last one to two years.

■ Fast Facts on Limiting CCA Exposure

Seal the wood at least every six months with standard penetrating deck treatments.

Replace sections with potential high exposure (handrails, steps, deck boards) with nonarsenic alternatives.

Wash your hands and your children's hands after every exposure to CCA-treated wood, especially before eating.

Keep children and pets away from the soil beneath and immediately surrounding arsenic-treated wood structures.

Cover arsenic-treated picnic tables with a tablecloth before using.

Do not pressure wash to clean the surface. Instead use a soap-and-water solution with disposable cleaning supplies. Pressurized water will blast off the upper surface of the wood and spray arsenic-contaminated particles over your yard. (Sanding the wood also spreads the particles.)

Do not allow children to play on rough wood surfaces; the splinters can be dangerous.

Never sand arsenic-treated lumber. If wood is smooth enough that splinters are not a risk, avoid sanding a deck to prepare the surface for sealing. Use a simple soap-and-water wash instead.

Do not store toys or tools under the deck. Arsenic leaches from the wood when it rains and may coat things left there.

Do not use commercial deck-washing solutions. They can convert chemicals on the wood to a more toxic form.

The biggest problem building a deck in the city is location. Gail and Henry wanted one, and the only available space was on their roof, so they hired a contractor to build one for them, including using composite material for decking. The couple knew that the construction would be expensive, but having recreational space in the city is well worth the investment. Because they live in a historic district, they had to endure a lengthy approval process that involved planning and zoning boards, the neighborhood association, and the historic commission.

"Despite the effort involved and the expense, it will give us a space to entertain or just sit in the sun watching the world go by," Gail said. "It also will be an advantage at resale time because decks are prized in this neighborhood, where there is very little open space."

A bilevel deck, built by a private contractor after the buyer had settled on this new house.

■ Fast Facts on Pressure Washers

There are cleanup jobs that require just a scrub brush and elbow grease. Then there are the really tough ones, such as removing layers of dirt from a concrete sidewalk or mildew from a wooden deck, that only a pressure washer can handle.

A pressure washer takes water from an outdoor faucet through a hose and focuses a high-pressure stream on whatever you're trying to clean. How much pressure you need depends on which jobs you plan to do. For light-duty jobs, such as washing the car or cleaning aluminum or vinyl siding or patio furniture, a washer with 1,300 to 2,000 pounds per square inch of pressure (psi) is enough. A medium-duty washer (2,000 to 2,600 psi) will dislodge dirt from a concrete sidewalk. Heavy-duty washers run from 2,600 to 4,000 psi, and are for stripping paint or removing stains from a concrete driveway.

Electric power washers typically produce up to 1,500 psi, only enough for lighter jobs. To avoid electric shock, have an electrician install a ground fault circuit interrupter (GFCI) on the outdoor outlet into which you'll plug the power washer; the GFCI will cut off the electricity if the power cord comes into contact with water. (As a general safety rule, all outdoor electrical outlets should have GFCIs.)

Medium- and heavy-duty washers typically are gasoline-powered, with five- or six-horse-power engines. They require the same kind of maintenance as gasoline-powered lawn mowers: You'll need to clean the air filter and change the spark plug and oil.

Power washers can run from $100 to $2,000, depending on the type and whether they are electric or gasoline powered. Electric units run $100 to $250. Gas-powered washers start at $250 and go up to about $2,000 for commercial models.

Here's a piece of bad advice: "Buying a pressure washer is more cost-effective than renting one." Most people need a pressure washer once or twice a year, if that often. It might be better to rent a washer for $50 to $75 a day to clean your deck, brick patio, or sidewalk than to spend $200 for something that just takes up space in the garage or basement.

Don't pressure-wash deteriorating stucco. The slightest pressure may further loosen the material, and water may get behind the stucco and seep into interior walls, putting your house at risk for mold development.

Some pressure-washing jobs—really big ones and high jobs come to mind—are better left to professionals. Never use a power washer while standing on a ladder unless a second person is available to help make sure the ladder is stabilized and the hose from the washer doesn't get tangled. Power washers, even light-duty ones, have a kick to them.

Experts debate the importance of pounds per square inch versus gallons per minute to pressure-washer use. Pounds per square inch is a measure of pressure applied to a job; for example, a rust stain on a concrete driveway might require a psi of 3,000 to dislodge. Gallons per minute (gpm) tells you how much of the driveway can be cleaned in a given time. Basically, the higher the gpm, the faster the washer will clean, allowing for the user's skill in handling it, of course.

■ PATIOS

As we've seen, decks are not the only choice homeowners have. More patios are being built nationwide than decks. If you plan ahead, depending on the size, you can build a patio in a weekend.

At least that's what some experts say, and why not? With the advent of interlocking concrete pavers and the continuing low cost of paving brick, hard-scaping, as this is often known, can be more of a do-it-yourself project than deck building.

A stone patio at the edge of a waveless swimming pool provides an ideal place for grilling (Photo courtesy of Fuego).

Not all bricks can be pavers. Paving brick, which is laid on a bed of sand, gravel, or mortar, is harder and more durable than the standard brick used in wall construction. Paving brick is known as SW, or severe weather, brick, and has a typical dimension of 8 by 4 by 2 1/4 inches.

Technology has provided a greater choice of pavers. More builders and homeowners are using interlocking concrete pavers for drive-ways, walkways, and patios. These pavers are machine-made, molded-concrete forms that come in a variety of shapes, colors, and pat-terns, allowing greater flexibility in design than rectangular bricks do. They also stay cleaner. Clay bricks hold moisture, so algae grows on them, and they need to be power-washed regu-larly. According to the experts, however, con-crete pavers do not hold moisture.

Interlocking pavers come in a variety of colors. Home centers generally carry 3 or 4 styles, but there are at least 40 that can be ordered. The pavers are typically smaller than bricks, so they lay more quickly. The interlocking tabs automatically create proper spacing and result in less shifting than you get with brick pavers.

A 4-by-20-foot walkway or 8-by-10-foot patio should take 8 to 12 hours, depending on skill. Installation time does not include removal of existing surfaces, such as grass and concrete walkways or patios, which can require demoli-tion. Getting to a proper foundation requires removing material 7 3/8 inches deep, because the pavers require a 4-inch base of crushed rock.

Try to prepare the site well in advance of paver installation. If you do the hard stuff first and take a break, laying the base and the pavers will seem easy and provide quick gratification.

A layer of concrete sand, called "double O," is used to fill out the base for the pavers. The sand has tiny pebbles in it.

Leveling and getting the patio or sidewalk to drain away from the house are two things that can drive do-it-yourselfers crazy. For proper drainage, you should pitch the patio or sidewalk three-quarters of an inch every four feet, although some do it an inch every four feet. To keep it level, you should use two one-inch-diameter pipes and run the screed, a board used to spread the crushed stone, in between them.

To make design easier, outline the dimensions with a garden hose. (This also works in garden and pond design.)

Working with pavers does not require many tools for the do-it-yourselfer other than safety glasses, a spade, gloves, and a push broom for the filler sand. To cut the pavers, and that is always necessary, use a brick chisel and a four-pound mallet. Draw a line on the brick and then score it with the edge of a cold chisel that has a blade wider than the brick face. Put the chisel on the score line and strike it with the mallet. The cut should be clean.

Because brick pavers are rectangular, designs are limited to three basic patterns: running bond, also called jack on jack; herringbone; and basketweave. Bricks can be used to create an overlapping-arc design, but getting the proper spacing is difficult. Bricks should have $1/8$ to $1/16$ inch of space between them to allow for expansion and contraction. Because brick pavers are the same size and shape, it is easier to estimate the number needed. The ratio is 4.75 bricks per square foot, so if you have a 100-square-foot project, you will need 475 bricks, plus 5 percent more for breakage.

With concrete pavers, the design dictates how many you will need. Dry-fit the pavers into a square foot, multiply the number by the total square footage, then add 5 percent to the total for mistakes.

Proper edging of brick paver walks and other surfaces reduces the chances of pavers shifting when you walk on them. Edging bricks, called sailors, are embedded vertically in a narrow trench around the perimeter, with the top of the sailor level with the pavers to be laid horizontally. Once the edging is completed, the bricks are laid from corner to corner. When all the brick pavers have been laid, sand or mason's silica is worked from the middle of the surface between the pavers with a broom. The bricks are then tamped to level the surface.

Interlocking paver installation is similar, except that you begin at the center and work out to the edges. Pavers that are cut should be in areas where they are not as noticeable. Edging material is usually installed after all the interlocking pavers have been laid. Sand is also used to fill in the joints, and a power tamper is a handy tool to make sure that the surface is level. Whatever you do, do not wash the excess sand off with a hose. The sand will eventually work itself between the joints.

The road to outdoor living is paved with, well, concrete pavers. Check out the latest in patio-making materials at www.remodelingonthemoney.com

Shelter from the Storm

"When we came back, we didn't know which houses had been damaged by the hurricane or had always been that way.**"**

—**New Orleans resident, on life after Katrina'**

13

David and Mary knew when they traded the Middle Atlantic for Florida 15 years ago that there might be a payback someday. After all, although Washington could be cold and snowy some winters, and the ocean could only be reached by a long drive on traffic-choked highways in the hot and humid summers, Florida was often in the path of hurricanes that have the potential to mow down everything in their path.

Fortunately, for most of those 15 years, their Palm Beach County home had been spared the brunt of the hurricanes and tropical storms that have made their way through Florida, including Hurricane Andrew, which pummeled Dade County south of Miami and led officials in Dade as well as the state to come up with codes designed to reduce costly damage that was pushing up homeowners' insurance rates so it was becoming unaffordable.

The respite ended in October 2005 when the city and Palm Beach County took a hit from Wilma, only the third Category 5 hurricane to strike Florida since the government began keeping records. The couple's house was damaged in its most vulnerable spots—the roof and the garage door—while electricity was lost for close to 20 days, increasing the potential for mold because air-conditioning helps dry out exposed wet areas quickly after a storm. The fence surrounding the house was blown down in high winds, as were ficus trees in their yard.

Because Hurricanes Katrina and Rita had ripped through the Gulf Coast slightly more than a month before, bringing with them media coverage of the havoc the storms had caused throughout New Orleans and the Mississippi coast, Wilma went practically unnoticed except in Florida, where it killed 35 people and caused about $13 billion in insured damages, practically ruined the citrus crop, and left the east coast of the state, especially Broward and Palm Beach Counties, in tatters.

Hurricane-force winds take out a garage door; one-car garages have smaller openings and stand up better.

"We decided to make some changes to prepare for the next one, which we know will come," Mary said. "Installing a new hurricane-resistant garage door is one of the ways we can try to limit the damage from wind and rain because that is the largest opening in the house and therefore the most vulnerable."

About 80 percent of residential hurricane wind damage starts with wind entry through the garage door. Studies have shown that hurricane winds exert the greatest pressure and suction at the corners of a structure, which is the location of most garage doors. A garage door is held in place only by the door's tracks. Hurricane winds exert both tremendous pressure and suction on the garage door, causing it to flex inward and outward.

Consequently, hurricanes generate severe stress not only on the door, but on its supporting tracks as well. As the pressure builds, the garage door pushes against and pulls away from the garage door tracks. If either the tracks or door give way, the garage door blows in or is sucked out. This allows the full power of the hurricane force winds to enter the compromised structure and attack the roof and walls.

Garage doors can now be constructed, tested, and rated for impact and wind resistance. The marginal cost of a rated garage door is only $200 to $300

A hurricane-resistant garage-door retrofit.

more than a door without wind-resistant features. A retrofit kit to strengthen an existing two-car garage door will cost about $300. A kit usually consists of a vertical post that is placed between the roof and the concrete floor, although other systems also exist. Single-car openings are more resistant to strong winds than two-car garage doors.

Windows are a major high-wind-vulnerable point in a house. Margaret had impact-resistant windows, manufactured by Simonton, installed in her house three months before Hurricane Wilma hit. The only damage was a few missing roof shingles.

"Our extended family stayed in our home watching the storm through these impact-resistant windows for five hours," Margaret said. "We saw the strong winds actually flex the glass in and out of the frame, but the windows held firmly in place."

Kathryn's Florida condo also took a direct hit in 2004 from Hurricane Ivan. The condo had minimal water damage from a neighbor's leaky roof, but that was it. The other units were so badly damaged that there was a chance that the entire building would be condemned. Again, impact-resistant windows, installed seven months before the storm, saved Kathryn's condo from her neighbors' fate. She had researched the windows and shared the information with other residents, but they considered the investment too expensive—a decision, she said, they now regret.

These windows cost more than energy-efficient windows. In chapter 9, it was noted that double-pane, low-emissivity windows added up to 3 percent of the cost of a 2,250-square-foot new house ($9,000 for a $300,000 house). According to the Federal Alliance for Safe Homes, the cost of impact-resistant glass in the same size house would be more than $14,000. Per-square-foot estimates, including frames, range from $30 to $55 installed.

Reinforced window glass is designed to stand up to high winds on the coast.

Impact-resistant windows are made from glass laminated with composites that provide enough strength to allow windows to withstand high winds and projectiles. This impact-resistant glazing can reduce the risk of window failure and personal injury or property loss during tornadoes, hurricanes, and explosions. When struck, laminated glass may crack or shatter, but the glass fragments tend to adhere to a plastic layer and stay in place.

Simonton StormBreaker windows are installed on new construction on the oceanfront. The windows can withstand hurricane force winds and flying projectiles (Photo courtesy of Simonton).

To meet code requirements, these windows have to undergo a series of tests. At Simonton, an air cannon shoots a 2-by-4 piece of lumber that's 9-feet long and weighs 9 pounds directly at a window. The piece of lumber is shot multiple times at both specific and varying parts of the same window at a rate of 50 feet per second. After numerous impacts, the units are then subjected to 9,000 cycles of combined positive and negative pressure.

> Some homeowners' insurance deductibles in Florida are often 2 to 5 percent, and 10 percent for mobile homes. After four hurricanes, you add the deductibles and you can't afford to rebuild.

> Enacting stronger building codes that specify use of concrete, steel, windows and doors that can withstand the impact of 2-by-4's propelled at 150 mph, and roofs anchored with hurricane clips, is one way that states, municipalities, and the construction industry are working together to reduce damage.

Overall, the windows are tested to withstand winds up to 146 miles per hour (mph) (a strong Category 4 hurricane). To achieve Dade County approval, each window needs to function operationally after having gone through all the testing.

Plywood is the material most homeowners tend to use to protect their windows during a hurricane. Pieces of plywood are the least expensive of the so-called "hurricane shutters," at $1 to $5 a square foot, and are typically a do-it-yourself project once a hurricane warning has been issued. Other hurricane shutters are made of acrylic or steel panels, and even roll up and down by the push of a button. These require a battery backup in case the power goes out before they roll down. Prices of the metal and acrylic shutters range from $25 to $60 a square foot, installed.

The strength of a material will determine how well a structure performs in a significant event such as high wind or an earthquake. There

Windows are tested at a lab to see if they will withstand hurricane-driven projectiles (Photo courtesy of Simonton).

are other variables to consider, too, such as how well those materials withstand stresses or strains, or, in the case of the Gulf Coast and Hawaii, termite infestation.

Moisture also has an effect on the materials, including rot and corrosion that weaken them. In addition, a structure begins to change after it is built, and the older it is, the less able it will be to withstand the kinds of stresses that a hurricane or flooding will create. A material is only as strong as the fasteners or connectors being used to join it. Any weakness will compromise the integrity of a structure.

How a building component is used and installed also determines how well a structure will hold up. If a material is difficult to work with, and the builder needs to finish the job quickly and is concerned about profit margin, the material might not be used properly, increasing the likelihood of its failing.

Simonton's StormBreaker Plus impact-resistant windows use a single-sheet of laminated glass developed for automobiles. The glass shatters, but the shards remain in place and the window stays whole.

Yet, while claims are made that certain materials, including steel, can handle winds in excess of 200 mph, what actually determines how well a structure withstands extreme events has less to do with the materials used than how the building is designed. A wood-frame house and a steel-frame house both can be designed to withstand winds of 200 mph. Many states and counties in high-risk areas have adopted "code-plus" programs, which use new basic building codes designed to reduce damage and fortify them with higher standards. This adds to construction costs, but the savings realized through lower insurance rates over time will likely pay for the increases.

Plywood, if properly installed, protects windows from high winds and projectiles.

In Massachusetts and New York, private insurance companies have canceled coverage for 80,000 coastal residents since 2004, even though it has been decades since a major hurricane struck the northeastern United States.

Depending on the remodeler's experience, steel framing can be more expensive than wood. Framing material and labor account for only 15 percent of total construction costs, and using steel adds $2,600 more to that expense for a 2,100-square-foot house. This translates, however, into an increase of only 1 percent in total construction cost. Concrete is used extensively in the South because of its ability to withstand insects, wind, and moisture. In the past few years, interlocking concrete forms (ICFs) have been used increasingly at construction sites all over the country. ICFs are used in the construction of "safe rooms" for houses that are considered at risk from high winds. ICFs have been shown to withstand winds from a Category 5 hurricane (155 mph). Testing has shown that an object such as a 15-pound 2-by-4 wood stud, when carried by 250 mph winds in a tornado, has enough force to penetrate most common building materials used today.

Insulated concrete forms have been shown to withstand hurricane force winds and stand up to storm surges (Photo courtesy of Greenblock).

A safe room, usually off a master bedroom, can double as a walk-in closet or a laundry room. If reinforced with eight inches of concrete, the room can withstand those 250 mph winds. When safe rooms are added as part of new construction, they can add $18,000 to the purchase price. There are no comparable figures for existing homes, although many homeowners along the Gulf Coast are including safe rooms in addition projects.

To protect occupants during a windstorm, the shelter has to be adequately anchored to the house foundation to resist overturning and uplift. The connections between all parts of the shelter must be strong enough to resist failure, and the walls, roof, and door must resist penetration by wind-borne objects.

Florida's state insurance pool has swelled to about 1.5 million policyholders.

Many manufacturers are focusing on keeping a home's occupants safe during a tornado or hurricane. DuPont has developed the StormRoom, engineered to specifications recommended by the Federal Emergency Management Agency. Room size ranges from 24 to 64 square feet, at a cost of $5,000 to $8,000.

DuPont uses its Kevlar-laminated sheathing—the same material used to make bulletproof vests—to create a room with walls that can stop a 15-pound, 12-foot wooden 2-by-4 picked up by a Category 5 (250 mph) tornado and propelled at 100 mph. According to DuPont, Kevlar is five times stronger than steel but weighs much less, allowing more design flexibility. The room was created in partnership with Simpson Strong-Tie of Dublin, California, which came up with an epoxy anchoring system that connects it with the foundation or concrete slab, making it resistant to wind uplift.

Wood framing is reinforced by light-gauge steel studs.

Windows are sealed to prevent moisture intrusion.

■ Fast Facts on Wind-Resistant Roofs

When replacing shingles, consider reinforcing the connection between the sheathing to the rafters and the trusses:

Remove the roofing material down to the sheathing.

Inspect and reinforce the rafter or truss connection to the walls.

Replace any damaged sheathing.

Nail the sheathing using ring-shank nails every six inches.

Seal the roof sheathing joints to provide additional moisture protection.

Existing houses can be retrofitted to better withstand high winds by securing roof sheathing to trusses when replacing roofs with hurricane-resistant clips and fasteners, using anchor straps for the foundation, and adding hurricane-resistant doors and impact-resistant windows—especially in houses that can't accommodate hurricane shutters.

ICFs are used to create a house; included will be a safe room that will provide storage and shelter from the storm.

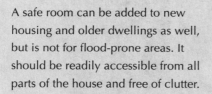

A safe room can be added to new housing and older dwellings as well, but is not for flood-prone areas. It should be readily accessible from all parts of the house and free of clutter.

Flooding, not wind, was the chief instrument of Hurricane Katrina's destruction along the Gulf Coast, and many replacement houses are being raised above flood- and storm-surge stage on pilings. Not that the idea of raising houses above flood level is a new one. Some older houses in New Orleans, for example, sit on brick pilings to get them off the ground. New construction sits on concrete slabs resting on telephone poles driven 18 to 20 feet into the bedrock, but because many of the city's houses were old, and some were not well-maintained, they were particularly hard-hit.

While it is less costly to build new than retrofit older houses to withstand hurricanes, the Florida Department of Financial Services is offering the "My Safe Florida Home" program to help qualified owners of existing houses pay

To prevent damage from flooding from storm surges, houses are built on pilings.

Damage from flooding devastated this kitchen.

for hurricane-resistance improvements that are recommended through a free home inspection. This is a matching grant of $5,000, and includes seven categories of possible improvements, including stronger roof decking, creating a secondary water barrier to prevent water intrusion, and reinforcing roof-to-wall connections and exterior-door upgrades. The state assumes that insurance companies will offer discounts on premiums to homeowners who make these improvements.

> Failure of a lockset, doorjamb, or hinges frequently causes exterior doors to blow inward. To prevent this, the deadbolt should penetrate the stud framing around the door, not just the doorjamb.

While most homeowners are focused on wind damage, the experts say that hail damage results in $1 billion in insurance claims each year. In response, Owens Corning and some other roofing shingle manufacturers have added reinforcement to the backs of their shingles, and have tested it by dropping two-inch steel balls onto the shingles from 30 feet up. The impact, many times more than that from a likely worst-case scenario, earned the Owens Corning shingle a Class 4 rating from Underwriters Laboratories—and, according to the National Association of Home Builders Research Center in Upper Marlboro, Maryland, that makes the shingle the most resistant to hail damage.

Generators provide electricity when the power is out.

Some major companies are offering discounts on homeowners' insurance premiums for using roofing products with a Class 4 rating. The trade-off is that these shingles often cost 50 percent more than standard ones.

Roofing shingles are being redesigned to meet wind-resistance requirements—up to 130 mph for some products—by increasing the performance of the sealant strip on the edges of the shingles. The industry standard requires that the strips be sealed at a temperature of 140 degrees, but some manufacturers have been able to get the sealing temperature down to 100 degrees.

> Commonsense techniques, such as adding extra nails or using heavier vinyl siding, are part of making houses hurricane resistant. When shingles are nailed, four nails are used instead of six. Heavier vinyl siding can withstand winds of 180 mph.

Damage from Hurricane Katrina to an historic building.

Windows are framed so that moisture intrusion is prevented during heavy rainstorms driven by wind (Photo courtesy of Simonton).

Sealing the shingles eliminates pockets into which the wind can find its way to blow them off.

Door manufacturers are putting their faith and a lot of research and development into the impact resistance of fiberglass exterior doors. Such doors make up only 12 percent of the market, and the reason is the word "fiberglass." Homeowners want their exterior doors to look like real wood as well as afford protection from storms, moisture intrusion, and insect infestation, including termites. Door manufacturers are using acrylic and vinyl finishes to create the appearance of and, in many cases, the feel of wood. Jeld-Wen's models were the product of a fiber-injection technology that combines fiberglass with polyester to make the doors four times stronger than what Jeld-Wen had been producing, according to the company. The process increases the fiberglass content of the door to 35 percent, from 10 to 12 percent.

The impact-resistance test was the Dade County code's 2-by-4 at 50 feet per second. The 2-by-4 simply bounced off the door.

The weather seems to be getting more unpredictable. See the latest on dealing with natural disasters at www.remodelingonthemoney.com

What *Is* That Smell?

14

Tom and Penny began to notice the funny smell in the basement just a few months after they moved into their century-old house. At first, the musty odor was limited to an area on the other side of the powder room near the old-style "rumpus" room by the front of the basement. Then they could easily detect that musty smell in the living room and dining room above.

Tom suspected moisture, so he bought a drywall saw and made a small hole in the wall where he and Penny had first detected the musty odor. Sure enough, on the inside of the wall, there was a leak in a drain line that carries waste from the kitchen to the soil pipe, and surrounding it on the foundation wall and the other side of the drywall was a black goo that smelled as if an animal had died.

A whole-house humidifier adds moisture through the heating system.

The leak, which was probably months old, was supporting the growth of black mold. While less common than other molds, this one—*Stachybotrys chartarum*—is more dangerous to humans because, given the proper environmental conditions, it can create multiple toxic chemicals called mycotoxins. These toxic by-products exist in the spores of the mold, as well as in the tiny fragments that can become airborne. Of particular concern is the threat that humans will inhale and ingest these toxic spores.

Tom and Penny had a plumber repair the leak, and then hired a mold remediation company to remove every last bit of the mold at a cost of about $1,500. Tom might have done the job himself, which required removing several square feet of drywall and replacing it, but decided that he would rather have it done properly than save a few dollars. Because their homeowners' insurance company no longer covers mold in the standard policy, Tom and Penny swallowed the expense.

Fortunately, the couple and their two children didn't appear to suffer any health problems related to the presence of this toxic mold in their house. The plumber suggested that the leak was as recent as a couple of months, but even he seemed surprised at how rapidly the mold had grown and filled the cavity around the drain line.

Mold cleanup can be painstaking. The sources of the mold have to be located, the areas have to be contained, and the material has to be removed under controlled circumstances, then vacuumed, washed, and vacuumed again. Drywall is porous, and if there's mold, it's all over the place. Hard furniture such as tables can be cleaned, but soft furniture such as couches have to be gotten rid of. Air tests are taken before the job begins and after it has been completed to determine the level of mold spores.

Mold thrives most often in moist conditions. Moisture combined with a nutrient source such as soil, dust, and products containing cellulose or other dead organic matter provide the ideal environment for colonization. Though indoor mold always has been a problem, it has been aggravated by changes in construction techniques brought on by the energy crisis of the 1970s. Efforts to create energy-efficient houses without accompanying efforts to regularly exchange the air inside have been linked to a dramatic increase in cases of asthma in the past three decades.

Not every mold is a potential hazard. Without mold, for

Mold fills a basement.

■ Fast Facts about Mold

Potential health effects associated with mold exposure include allergic reactions, asthma, and other respiratory complaints.

There is no practical way to eliminate all mold and mold spores indoors. The way to control indoor mold growth is to control moisture.

Reduce indoor humidity (by 30 to 60 percent) by venting bathrooms, dryers, and other moisture-generating sources to the outside; using air conditioners and dehumidifiers; increasing ventilation; and using exhaust fans whenever cooking, dishwashing, and cleaning.

Clean and dry any damp or wet building materials and furnishings within 24 to 48 hours to prevent mold growth.

Clean mold off hard surfaces with water and detergent, and dry completely. Absorbent materials, such as ceiling tiles, that are moldy may need to be replaced.

Prevent condensation. Reduce the potential for it on cold surfaces (including windows, piping, exterior walls, roof, or floors) by adding insulation.

In areas where there is a perpetual moisture problem, do not install carpeting (for instance, near sinks or on concrete floors with leaks or frequent condensation).

Molds can be found almost anywhere; they can grow on virtually any substance, providing moisture is present.

A basement dehumidifier set at 40 percent.

instance, all cheese would taste the same, and we'd have no penicillin. Still, some segments of the population, such as asthmatics, are more sensitive to certain kinds of mold, especially when it is airborne. According to the Centers for Disease Control and Prevention, there are few case reports that toxic molds inside homes can cause unique or rare health conditions such as pulmonary hemorrhage or memory loss. A causal link between the presence of a toxic mold and these conditions has not been proven.

Mold is just one of the indoor pollutants that experts say is affecting our health. In our push for efficient use of energy, we have made houses so tight they can't breathe. As a result, we can't breathe well, either. A growing body of scientific evidence indicates that the air in houses and other buildings can

■ Fast Facts on Indoor Pollutants

The following are some pollutants that may be found in the home:

Respirable particles: found in fireplaces, woodstoves, and kerosene heaters

Organic pollutants: from household products including paints and paint strippers, wood preservatives, aerosol sprays, cleansers, and disinfectants

Formaldehyde: found in hardwood plywood wall paneling, particleboard and fiberboard, urea-formaldehyde foam insulation (now banned), durable press drapes, other textiles, and glues

Pesticides: from insecticides and termite treatments; lawn and garden products that are tracked into the house

Lead: from automobile exhausts seeping in from garages, sanding or burning lead-based paint, lead solder (now banned in plumbing)

Asbestos: found in deteriorating insulation and fireproofing

Biological pollutants: caused by wet or moist walls, ceilings, and carpets; poorly maintained humidifiers, dehumidifiers, and air conditioners; household pets

Carbon monoxide and nitrous dioxide: from unvented kerosene and gas heaters; leaking chimneys and furnaces; down-drafting from woodstoves and fireplaces; all gas stoves

Radon: from earth, uranium, and rock beneath some homes; well water; and building materials

be more seriously polluted than outdoor air in the largest and most industrialized cities.

The problem of indoor air quality has become more widespread as we have sought ways to reduce the amount of energy we use to heat and cool our houses. As buildings became tighter and less able to breathe, we also began spending more time indoors—working longer hours, spending more time with our families, needing security in a less-secure world.

Research indicates that people spend about 90 percent of their time indoors. Thus, for many, the risks to health may be greater because

Moisture creates mushrooms on a basement wall.

Cleanup of pollutants requires rooms to be sealed off.

of exposure to air pollution indoors. What is worse is that the people who might be affected most by indoor pollution often cannot escape their environment. These include the very young and the elderly, but especially the chronically ill suffering from respiratory or cardiovascular disease.

The primary causes of indoor air-quality problems are sources of pollution that release gas or particles into the air. Outdoor air must be brought into a house to dilute emissions and carry these pollutants outside where they can dissipate. High temperatures and high levels of humidity also can increase the levels of pollutants.

Sources of indoor pollution include combustion sources such as oil, gas, kerosene, coal, wood, and tobacco. Since the 1950s, residential builders have used more manufactured products in construction and remodeling. Plywood, adhesives, and a host of home furnishings such as carpets and drapes are manufactured with thousands of chemicals.

Low VOC paints reduce the indoor air pollution.

Air from the outdoors can enter a house three ways: infiltration (through cracks in the walls and joints in floors); natural ventilation (open doors and windows); and mechanical ventilation (outdoor-vented fans such as those in range hoods in kitchens and in bathrooms, as well as whole-house systems that remove indoor air and distribute filtered air through the house).

So can central air-conditioning solve your moisture and ventilation problems? Most central air-conditioning systems are not sized properly for the house and they do not run all the time, kicking in when they are needed. A better answer

■ Fast Facts on Room Air Cleaners

Airtight construction and close-fitting windows and doors save energy and lower fuel costs. But an unexpected consequence is bad air quality. Opening a window won't help much unless you can exchange all the air in the room every hour. Buying the right air cleaner, however, might.

The higher the level of tobacco smoke, pollen, and dust in a room, the faster an air cleaner must work to clean it, so buy one that can handle the job. The Clean Air Delivery Rate, or CADR, indicates the volume of filtered air the unit can deliver. Room size ratings are calculated based on the removal of at least 80 percent of smoke and other particles in a steady-state room environment, assuming one air change per hour with complete mixing in the room. For example, a 120-square-foot room requires an air cleaner with a CADR of at least 80, assuming an 8-foot ceiling. The higher the ceiling, the larger the rating needed.

Be sure to ask what kind of pollutants the air cleaner's filter is designed to handle best. If you suffer from pollen-related allergies, for example, you'll want a filter that removes the greatest amount of pollen possible. Remember: Tobacco odors are produced by gases and are not completely removed by any filter.

Room model purifiers that can clean the air in an entire room can cost $180 to $1,000; tabletop units that clean smaller areas run from $60 to $180 and are often designed to clear tobacco smoke in the immediate area of a smoker. The room units do a better job overall.

There is some debate about whether cleaners are the answer for people with allergies triggered by larger particles such as house dust allergens, some molds, and animal dander. Most of these are found on surfaces, according to the U.S. Environmental Protection Agency. They cannot be removed by an air cleaner unless disturbed and re-suspended in the air.

Good advice: Help the unit do its job by vacuuming thoroughly, reducing clutter, and cleaning surfaces where dust and mold gather. Above all, change the air filter according to the instructions.

Jargon alert: HEPA (High Efficiency Particulate Air) filters trap 99.97 percent of all airborne pollutants 0.3 micron or larger from the air passing through the filter. That will usually take care of most pollutants. Some machines (ozone cleaners and ionizers) introduce small amounts of ozone into the air to reduce pollutants, but ozone can be a lung irritant, too.

is to have a dehumidifier running from June to November, but be sure to clean the filter regularly and get rid of the water—poorly maintained dehumidifiers can work against you.

To improve the indoor environment, healthy houses have a central mechanical ventilation system supplying fresh filtered air, a sealed and balanced duct system, high-efficiency filters, and interior design choices that minimize dust collection and volatile organic compounds.

Then there is controlled indoor humidity. Ideal humidity in cold-climate houses is 40 to 60 percent. Higher humidity encourages dust mite and mold growth; lower levels increase the spread of respiratory infections. Ideal humidity levels are achieved by a balanced ventilation system with sources of excessive moisture eliminated or minimized. Finally, energy and resource efficiency reduces condensation and improves ventilation, eliminating the infiltration of sometimes toxic air into the home.

The effects of indoor pollution can be experienced soon after exposure or years later.

Immediate effects could include eye, nose, and throat irritation; headaches; dizziness; and fatigue. Immediate effects are short term and treatable in most cases.

Because most of us are not trained medical personnel, we often assume that we are sick for the wrong reasons. Studies in the 1990s, for example, showed that many people seeking emergency-room treatment for prolonged respiratory illnesses in the winter actually were suffering from extended exposure to carbon monoxide caused by poorly maintained heating systems. By controlling relative humidity in a home, the growth of some biological contaminants can be minimized.

Relative humidity of 30 to 50 percent is generally recommended, but sometimes the interior of the house can be too dry. One of the best ways to control humidity levels, especially in the dry, northern winters, is by using a humidifier in a room or a whole-house unit attached to the furnace.

(Left) Mold created by flooding was eradicated by stripping the house to the studs.

(Above) Waterproofing is sprayed on the exterior wall of a foundation.

■ Fast Facts on Freestanding Humidifiers

Freestanding humidifiers come in two styles: consoles or cabinets, which sit on the floor, and smaller portable units that are easier to move and can sit on desks. Some models have adjustable fan speeds, built-in humidistats (which regulate the moisture), and automatic shutoffs in case the unit tips or the tank empties.

In either consoles or cabinets, you can find ultrasonic humidifiers, which create a cool mist by means of ultrasonic vibrations produced by a nebulizer that vaporize water particles. These units are fairly quiet.

There also are impellers, which produce a cool mist using a high-speed rotating disk. Evaporative units add moisture by using a fan to blow air through a moist, absorbent material, such as a filter or a wick (a porous pad). Steam vaporizers heat water using an electric element. A warm-mist humidifier is a kind of steam vaporizer, except that it produces cooled steam.

Ask about the drawbacks of each kind of humidifier, because all you want to do is add moisture to the air, not create an environmental hazard. You want a unit that won't raise indoor humidity levels above 35 percent in cold weather; anything more produces condensation on windows and walls that can breed mold and mildew. You don't want a unit that will spew minerals and microorganisms into the air.

Government tests show ultrasonic and impeller humidifiers require constant cleaning to prevent microorganisms from growing in the tanks of standing water then being dispersed into the air. High-end models come with antibacterial protection (an ultraviolet light, for example). Others come with replaceable cartridges that filter out minerals, which sometimes appear as a white dust in the air or as residue. Although evaporative humidifiers and steam vaporizers have tanks, they tend to introduce fewer pollutants into the air. The filters and wicks of high-end evaporative models are treated with antimicrobial products that reduce such buildup.

One drawback of traditional steam vaporizers is the danger that the steam will burn a child. Plus, they use more electricity than cool-mist ultrasonic and impeller units. Humidifier capacity is listed in gallons; that is, how many gallons of water are released into the air in 24 hours. To determine the capacity you need, calculate the volume of the space by multiplying the total floor area in square feet by the ceiling height. For 500 square feet or less, a 1 1/2- to 2-gallon-capacity humidifier is suitable. For 2,000 square feet, a capacity of 10 gallons or more is required.

**Need a humidifier that's right for your needs but won't empty your wallet?
Go shopping at www.remodelingonthemoney.com**

■ Fast Facts on Freestanding Humidifiers (*Continued*)

Prices range from $25 to $250, with portables at the lower end, and console models at the higher end. Cheaper units tend to be less effective.

Air cleaners for Rheem HVAC systems.

The cost of building a healthy house remains 25 percent higher than the cost of building a conventional home, but the savings in long-term medical costs make it worth it, advocates say. Homeowners, builders, and researchers are just now beginning to grasp the concepts involved. As more is learned about indoor pollution, construction techniques will become more universal and the costs will drop.

Ideas That Will Really Floor You

"The first question a buyer asks is 'What's under the carpet?'"

—Mark Wade, developer, investor, and real estate broker

15

This is not an exercise in rug-bashing. There is absolutely nothing wrong with properly installed and well-cared-for wall-to-wall carpet. Carpeting—especially the indoor-outdoor variety—is, in the words of Mike, "perfect for the basement, where the boys and their friends can hang out and watch television."

Carpeting, in this case a commercial-grade, Stainmaster product, was Sam and Lisa's choice for a runner on the stairs from the first to the second floor of their tiny late-19th century city townhouse. "Because I was a week away from having the twins, I needed something that would be soft and, with twins, easy to clean," Lisa said. "I just called the installer, picked a color, and headed for the hospital."

While favoring carpeting for the basement, Michael and Eileen had the carpeting removed from their family room and replaced it with laminate flooring. Why? Because they were living with the previous owners' tastes. The carpeting was wearing in a lot of places—the result of homeowners skimping on the padding underneath. Even the standard, everyday carpeting made today—most of it produced cheaply abroad—can last for many years if

No matter how dry your basement, always install indoor/outdoor carpeting manufactured with an additive to deter mold growth. Carpeting made of polypropylene is the moisture-resistant variety. Make sure there is a moisture barrier between the concrete floor and carpet padding.

Bamboo flooring is a renewable resource and comes in a growing number of colors.

Basketweave tile was popular in bathrooms from the turn of the 20th century and for several decades thereafter. Replacement tile is available on the Internet.

The typical width of carpet runner is 28 inches. Carpet is usually priced and sold by the square yard; all other flooring by the square foot. Carpet prices start at $8 a yard, uninstalled. Installation per yard starts at $6. Removing the old carpeting (the old padding, especially when super-stapled to the floor, is the biggest expense because it is so time-consuming) starts at about $3 per yard.

manufacturers' cleaning directions are followed and the padding is of adequate composition and thickness. In that way, people will get tired of the color or the stains long before the carpeting wears out.

■ LAMINATE FLOORING

"We like the laminate," Michael said. "It looks good, it is easy to care for, and everything I've read about it says that it will stand up to wear." Some laminate flooring comes with 10- to

15-year "durability" warranties, which guarantee that the surface will hold up to normal wear and tear, not fade in the sunshine, and not stain permanently. The warranty can be voided if the laminate is installed in an unusually wet area, such as a basement. Some building codes prohibit laminate flooring in basements or on concrete slabs because of moisture issues.

Tongue and groove laminate flooring is easy to install (Photo courtesy of Armstrong Flooring).

Lisa and Sam went the ceramic-tile route in their kitchen, and installed a marble floor in their first-floor powder room. Lisa did both jobs—the kitchen in one eight-hour day, and the marble floor in a morning.

"I went to the home center and watched a demonstration by an 86-year-old tile man, and then went home and did the job," said Lisa, who

> The thicker the padding, the longer the wear. Be careful of offers of free padding because "free" sometimes means lower quality. Thicker can cost $4 to $5 per square foot, but is a smart investment for first-time buyers on a tight budget. Thicker padding is also easier on the feet.

Quarry tile has commercial applications mostly, but is perfect for kitchen floors.

was seven months pregnant at the time. "When I did the bathroom, I had to rent an electric tile cutter, and the man was so impressed that this 'girl' was going to cut marble, he didn't charge me."

■ Fast Facts on Laminate Flooring:

There are two kinds: direct-pressure laminate fused together with heat and pressure, and high-pressure laminate in which pieces are glued and compressed with heat. A tough aluminum-oxide wear layer sits on top of a decorative paper impregnated with melamine—the so-called "image" layer that gives the floor its color or pattern, be it stone or wood grain. Several additional layers of resin-treated Kraft paper are added to high-pressure flooring for greater impact resistance. The core is made of high-density fiberboard. All of it sits on a backer material of nondecorative, high-pressure laminate that is designed to stabilize the product and to prevent moisture from wicking up through the back.

The thicker the flooring, the denser the core, the more durable, and the higher the price, from $2.00 to $5.50 a square foot; installation costs $3.00 a square foot. Laminate can be installed over concrete and radiant floor heating, and directly over any existing floor except carpet. Because laminate tends to echo when you walk on it, you should install a subfloor that provides a sound barrier. The most common method of installation of tongue-in-groove flooring is with a special glue to join the sections until the floor is covered. There are glueless floors, and they can come in exotic styles such as slate and Brazilian cherry.

Tastes change almost daily, and today's styles can be passé by 12:01 AM tomorrow. Unlike 150 years ago, when most houses had wood floors because carpeting was handmade and only available to the well-to-do, today's homeowners are faced with so many choices and, thus, so many more opportunities to make wrong decisions.

Laminate flooring can be made to look like tile. This flooring is glued rather than nailed to the subfloor.

Inexpensive "single-rail" manual cutters ($19 to $39) are fine for halving larger tiles, but intricate cuts and trims require an electric "wet" tile saw that is quick and precise. Unless you plan to tile the whole house, rent one at the home center for a few hours. Reduce rental time by marking cuts in advance, then "dry fitting" the tile quickly once all the cuts have been made. Cleaning the machine is time-consuming, but most rental places levy a hefty fee if they have to do it.

One installation caveat on carpeting: If you've ever smelled carpet glue, you know why you should install it when the weather is warm, so you can ventilate easily. Fortunately, the glue has lost a lot of its odor, thanks to the carpeting industry's success in reducing the level of volatile organic compounds in the adhesive.

Should you tile? Will that tile be ceramic, porcelain, marble, stone, or mosaic? What about a slate floor? What about the subfloor? Hardwood? Prefinished or unfinished? Sustainable or "green" flooring such as bamboo or cork? Laminate? Parquet? If vinyl is your price range, will it be sheet or tile? What about carpeting?

Change can be good, and flooring remains high on the homeowners' list of things to alter. The Remodelers Council of the National Association of Homebuilders, using U.S. Census Bureau data from 1994 to 2005, says that spending on flooring accounts for as little as $522 million (2003) and as much as $1.68 billion (1997) in a year.

■ TILE FLOORS

Louis and Janet weren't looking as much for change as they were a "midcourse correction" when they retiled the hallway and the half bath some years back.

A confluence of three different materials: Carpet, quarry tile hearth, and yellow pine.

"When we had our house built 19 years ago, we ran out of money, but we wanted to upgrade some of the flooring," Janet said. "Ceramic tile was the natural choice for us, we asked lots of questions, chose the tile, and did the floors in two half baths and the hallway ourselves. After a few years passed, however, we discovered that one of the most important parts of laying tile was choosing the correct grade of tile for the area that you are covering, particularly in high-traffic areas where it has to stand up to kids, dogs, and life in general."

It wasn't that the tile was turning to dust, but "the floor in front of the vanity had become scratched and worn," Janet said. "In the hallway, the dog, as well as constant traffic, had scratched the tile. Although it wasn't extreme damage, it really annoyed me to look at it when I cleaned the floors."

Janet wanted to redo the floors but, recalling all the work involved the first time, she was sure that Louis wouldn't go for it.

"I decided to talk to him about it right after waking one Saturday morning, before getting out of bed," she said. "I said I'd been toying with the idea of changing the tile, and what did he think? I braced myself, but when he spoke, he said something like, 'Yeah, we could do that....' I imagined I was still asleep and dreaming, but when I realized I was, indeed, awake, I sprang

> Tile contractors typically charge $6.50 per square foot to install ceramic tile. Marble and natural stone floors are more labor-intensive, so can run from $8.00 to $10.00 a square foot for installation. Depending on the type and style, floor tile can cost as little as 98 cents a square foot for the plain-vanilla variety, to as much as $20.00 a square foot for specialty tile.

A wet bed is the traditional subfloor for ceramic tile floors.

from the bed, ran downstairs, grabbed a crowbar, and began demolition before he realized what he had said and changed his mind."

It wasn't an easy demolition, especially removing the adhesive from the subfloor, Janet said, but "we picked a more durable tile for those results, and the end result is something we have lived with for at least 10 years. No visible signs of wear, and all is well."

◼ Fast Facts on Tile and Tiling

Porcelain tile is the newer kid on the block. It is made of finer clays and fired at much higher temperatures than ceramic, making the tiles denser, stronger, and less porous—meaning they are less prone to moisture and staining. They are a better, but pricier, choice for heavily trafficked areas; yet their durability compensates for the cost difference. It is much less commercial looking than quarry tile and is as durable.

Premixed adhesive and grout can only be spread over small areas at a time before they set and harden. Mixing your own grout and adhesive lets you spread both over larger areas. You also can control the amount of stain- and mildew-resistant additives that can alter consistency.

If you're hiring a tiling contractor, remember the following: A good job is all about details. Bargain-basement pricing usually means a rush job. A good contractor will snap out gridlines over the entire space to be tiled and then set up the entire area to see how the tile fits and looks.

Tile comes in various grades, and how and where you use the tile determines the kind of material you choose. No matter how expensive the tile is, it's the quality of installation that matters.

If you don't get 30 years out of a tiled floor, the contractor has done something wrong. The best subfloor for tile is the wet bed, but few contractors do it because it is labor-intensive and expensive. A wet bed increases the weight, but the standard house can support it. A 1-inch-deep wet bed in a 200- to 400-square-foot kitchen won't be too heavy, and because it puts even pressure on the entire floor, it will eliminate squeaks.

The size of the tiles is determined by the area. Big rooms can accommodate 12-by-12-inch tiles, but the big tiles can overwhelm a smaller space. Bigger tiles involve more cutting.

To prevent staining, seal the grout once a year. To clean, use warm water and mild detergent. For stubborn spots, white vinegar and a hot water solution works well. Be careful, however, because white vinegar will take the finish off slate and marble.

Never use exterior plywood as a subfloor. The job will last two years before moisture makes it fall apart. If you don't do a wet bed, use tile backer board instead. A 3-by-5-foot sheet of backer board, five-sixteenths of an inch thick, costs $10. Screw or nail the backer board to the floor joists every 8 inches so the backer board won't move and start to crumble.

You can change the color of the grout with epoxy stains. You can't make a dark color light, but you can make a light color dark. The stains also act as a sealant.

Watch a floor tile installation project from start to finish at www.remodelingonthemoney.com

■ WOOD FLOORS

The National Association of Home Builders surveys of potential buyers of new construction show that most prefer hardwood floors—primarily oak—in the entry foyer, dining room, and living room; tile or marble in the kitchen and bathroom; and carpeting on the stairs and in the bedrooms. There was a time when no one in his or her right mind would put wood floors in the bathroom or the kitchen, fearing moisture damage and warping, but there have been major

Sanding yellow pine is easy, and oiling where you've sanded can bring out the old floor.

improvements in home building techniques and wood treatments, including catalyzed sealers such as baked-on finishes that chemically bond to the wood to prevent moisture penetration. In addition, quick-curing, water-based polyurethane finishes can withstand dampness while maintaining the flexibility to accommodate wood's natural expansion and contraction.

> The owner of an investment property tore out the wall-to-wall carpeting, installed hardwood floors, and was able to get $300 more a month in rent because of it.

Despite the advances, most hardwood is still destined for living rooms and dining rooms. Gus and Joan decided to go with laminate in the 100-year-old townhouse they'd just put on the market, but put in oak flooring in the newer

Hardwood flooring has found its way into the kitchen, thanks to baked-on finishes and quick curing polyurethanes that can withstand dampness and still let wood expand and contract.

and larger 50-year-old detached, single-family house they'd just bought and renovated.

"There was carpet on the floor of our first house when we bought it and, after 10 years, I thought about taking off the old carpet and buying new," Gus said. "When I pulled up the carpet and started taking off the padding, there was all of this dust. I asked myself: 'What are we breathing in here?' and that's when I decided to go with hardwood flooring. We put in laminate flooring—stapled instead of glued. When we bought the new house, there was no question. It was going to be tongue-and-groove oak flooring instead of carpeting."

The new flooring went on top of the original quarter-inch flooring underneath the carpeting. "The old floor was nailed directly to the joists, just as all flooring was in the old days," Gus said. (New houses primarily have plywood subfloors'). "The

Cork flooring is easy on the feet, and appropriate for exercise rooms.

old floor was level, so we were able to put the new flooring right on top of it. We also decided to go with prefinished rather than unfinished flooring because we didn't want to have to deal with the stain and having to polyurethane the floors, too. The new flooring was angle stapled to the old floor and nailed at the edges. Those nail holes were filled in. We removed the baseboards and installed new ones and finished to match the color of the floor because the old ones had many coats of paint. Even if we were able to strip the paint down to the original wood, we didn't know whether it would be in good condition or if we could restain the old wood to match the color of the new floor. And we went with our own baseboards.

> The preference for hardwood flooring over carpeting is often health related. People have allergies to dust mites, and you are more likely to find those in carpets than in wood.

The flooring company makes baseboards that match, but they are so expensive. So I found baseboards the same thickness and mixed two different stains—golden walnut and a reddish stain—and was able to match the floor."

Gus and Joan's 1,300-square-foot floor took four days to install. The prefinished tongue-in-groove cost $3.45 a square foot. Gus received a discount of 45 cents per square foot

Hardwood stairs stand up to wear and tear better than yellow pine.

for buying in bulk, just as he did when he bought the laminate flooring for the old house, paying $2.35 per square foot versus the $2.65 full price— "because if you buy from a dealer, they are willing to discount if you look like you are ready to walk away from a sale."

Mark Wade, the real estate broker and investor, recently bought a 456-square-foot condo unit in a low-rise building to either flip or rent.

"So far, I've spent $900 to gut the place, and that included taking out about 400 square feet of old and ugly carpet and padding," Mark said. "What I'll do now is replace the carpeting with 400 square feet of hardwood flooring, which will cost about $10 a square foot for the flooring, installation, stain, and sealing, for a total of $4,000. I'll use a dark walnut stain and a high-gloss polyurethane that will bounce the light around. And, from experience, I'll guarantee you that I will get much more than $4,000 back when I sell the place."

> Areas of high visibility require great care in color choices. Some builders and homeowners use prefabricated materials; sometimes the dark cherrywood for the floor comes from one source and the baseboard and chair rail from another source, and they might not match.

■ Fast Facts on Hardwood Flooring

When installing a subfloor, use American Plywood Association–approved, under-layment grade plywood one-half inch or thicker. Do not use cheaper particleboard because it deteriorates over time, especially if there are moisture issues.

Hardwood flooring comes in several different widths and grades.

Strip flooring is typically narrow pieces of wood up to 2¾ inches wide. Plank flooring is wider, generally up to 7 inches.

Some wood, such as maple and birch, is ranked as "first, second, or third."

Oak is the most popular hardwood choice. It is judged as clear (few flaws); select bright grain, a few flaws, and most pieces match well.

No. 1 Common has light and dark pieces and some marks.

No. 2 Common allows for all character marks, such as knots, worm holes, and discoloration.

Unfinished wood is susceptible to swelling if it gets too much moisture.

Prefinished flooring costs more and colors are limited. Because the surface isn't sanded after installation, it might not be as smooth as the end result of unfinished flooring.

Hardwood flooring prices start as low as $4 a square foot, and installation runs about $5 per square foot.

What's the most durable and cost-effective wood flooring for your house? What you need to know is at www.remodelingonthemoney.com

(Above) A metal strip holds down the edge of the carpet.

(Left) Carpet choices include a growing number of products with low volatile organic compounds.

Don't forget the new kids on the wood flooring block: sustainable or "green" materials, primarily bamboo and cork flooring. Bamboo has been used as a flooring material in North America for about 10 years, and the most common is the Moso variety. It is now available in about 50 colors. While bamboo can grow 40 to 50 feet in about 6 months, the grass takes about 5 years to mature to a point at which it can be harvested and milled for flooring. It also has a water content of about 15 percent, meaning that, as with many other kinds of flooring, it needs to spend at least 24 hours in the room in which it is to be installed to become acclimated. Bamboo flooring starts about $6.25 a square foot, uninstalled, and installation costs are similar to those of laminate. It, too, comes prefinished as well as unfinished.

Cork flooring is resilient, meaning that it is easy on the feet when you've been standing for a long time, it is a good soundproofing material, an insulator, and resists mold and mildew. Cork flooring tiles are made from bark peeled from cork oak trees. It is also fire resistant and costs from $2.50 to $4.00 a square foot, uninstalled. Installation costs are about the same as laminate.

Another wood flooring choice was used by Scott, who chose engineered rather than

Carpeting protects the stairway and is quieter walking on when others are sleeping.

solid wood flooring for the kitchen and adjacent family room when he built the addition to his house. Engineered products, available in planks and strips, are manufactured of hardwood using a cross-directional laminated construction (three to five layers), with a top layer of premium hardwood. This construction counteracts the natural tendency of wood to expand and contract with seasonal changes in temperature and humidity, making engineered products dimensionally stable. The urethane coating makes it an option for high-moisture, high-traffic areas.

"I stapled it to the subfloor, and it went in fairly easily," said Scott, who installed the floor himself and shared construction duties for the entire 1,500-square-foot, two-story addition with a contractor and his assistant. "I did hit a snag around the base of the kitchen island, which already had been installed, but, with some judicious cutting, it worked out so the imperfection is barely noticeable. The dark flooring reflects the light shining through six windows on either side of the floor, so unless I confessed to the fudging, you'd never notice it."

Prices for engineered flooring start at $3 a square foot, and installation costs $5 a square foot, the same as regular hardwood flooring.

■ CARPETING

Carpeting appears to be getting a bad rap, but you have to remember something: Flooring replacement is a manifestation of homeowners' needs to make changes in their living space to reflect their personal tastes, and much of what is being changed is carpeting for other kinds of materials. A survey by the National

Carpeting was removed from this yellow pine flooring; the underlayment was stapled to the floor, and removing the staples damaged it.

Association of Home Builders shows that buyers are typically not wildly enthusiastic about whatever flooring they have been used to, although people with hardwood floors are happier than those with carpeting. Only 15 percent of buyers whose previous houses had wall-to-wall carpeting said they were "very satisfied" with the choice, while 26 percent of those with hardwood floors said they were happy with them.

■ Fast Facts on Carpeting

Before purchasing carpet, you need to answer the following questions: How is the room going to be used? Will it have heavy or light traffic? Will the room be the center of activity for family and entertaining? Is there direct access from the outside, or will the carpet be away from entrances? Will the carpet receive direct sunlight?

Where there is to be heavy traffic (usually the family room, hallways, and stairways), choose the best carpet you can afford.

When shopping for carpet, look for performance rating guidelines among the different brands. This rating system offers guidance on choosing the carpet that will perform best for various traffic needs. Most guidelines will be based on a 5-point scale, with a 4 or 5 rating being best for the highest traffic areas. A 2 or 3 rating is good for areas with less traffic.

To determine the approximate quantity of carpet you will need, multiply the length (feet) of the room by its width (feet) for the square footage. To obtain the square yardage, divide that figure by nine. Your retailer may figure the amount in square feet or square yards. Add 10 percent to account for room irregularities and pattern match. It is best to have your retailer or installer make final measurements to ensure that you purchase the correct amount. As professionals, they know how to include hallways and closets, match patterns, plan seam placement, work with room irregularities, and account for rooms with widths greater than 12 feet. (Most carpet is produced in 12- and 15-foot widths.)

Nylon is the most popular material. Wool is expensive; acrylic looks like wool but costs less. Polyester is easy to clean and resists stains. Olefin also resists stains and is easy to clean, is the stuff of which indoor/outdoor carpeting is made, and comes in various blends.

In general, carpeting runs from $27 to $60 a square yard installed, including padding. Outdoor carpeting runs about $14 a square foot.

With carpeting, daily vacuuming is the most important cleaning activity, but deep extraction cleaning must be performed to remove stubborn or embedded soil. Carpet should be dry- or wet-extraction cleaned a minimum of every 12 or 18 months before it shows soiling. Professional cleaning typically costs $35 to $50 a room.

■ VINYL FLOORING

We haven't said much about vinyl flooring, which is an inexpensive alternative to just about any other kind of material except carpeting. Because building codes in many municipalities around the country don't allow any material but vinyl and tile in bathrooms and kitchens, and vinyl remains popular, if a

Laminate flooring simply snaps into place
(Photo courtesy of Armstrong Flooring).

homeowner can afford it, he or she will replace the vinyl with granite or marble in the bathroom.

One of the chief attributes of vinyl—other than the reasonable price of the material—is the ease with which anyone with common sense can install it. For example, if vinyl sheeting is being installed as part of a kitchen addition, you should try to install the flooring while the kitchen is empty and then cover the space with cardboard or plastic so that reconstruction efforts don't nick or damage the vinyl.

Vinyl tile also is a little easier to work with. Typically, the tiles are 12 by 12 inches, trim very easily, and should be laid out in the same way that ceramic floor tiles are done—snapping chalk lines and then laying out all the tiles to see how they fit and where they'll need to be trimmed. The work should be done from the center out to the edges, where the trims are made.

Vinyl tile and sheet flooring can start as low as 88 cents per tile, and installation costs run about $1.50 a square foot. Tiles typically come in cartons of 20 or 30; sheeting comes on rolls. Expect to pay about $8.00 a square foot for materials and installation.

■ SANDING

If you're looking for a way to make your floors look new again, consider sanding. Ellen was looking for inexpensive ways to make her house more saleable in a market with too many houses for sale, and decided to rip up the carpeting in the living room, dining room, and second-floor bedrooms. Instead of following the usual route of hiring a refinisher or renting a floor sander, Ellen used a hand sander and did the work on her hands and knees.

"It was kind of fun, and I oiled the floors and they looked nice," she said. "The prospective buyers remarked on how they looked, and, while I didn't have as much luck with the floors in the bedrooms as I did on the first floor, this

> Many tiles have a self-adhesive that only requires peeling off the backing and sticking them down. Tiles without the backing require spreading an adhesive over the floor with a notched trowel, then setting the tiles. Vinyl tiles do have a few drawbacks. They have more edges and don't have a felt backing that sets in glue, so they may come loose easier than sheet vinyl. Frequent cleaning with water-based products can soak more moisture into the tiles. The cracks between tiles gather dust and debris that's hard to clean out.

If you have longleaf yellow pine floors, hang on to them. Yellow pine is so rare that what is available on the market is mainly lumber salvaged from the floors of demolished factories and warehouses in older cities.

is where the buyers notice more because this is the first place they see, and it becomes more of a memory point than a lot of other places in the house."

"Pumpkin pine" is a white pine found in many older houses, and is so called because working with it was as easy as cutting a pumpkin. What is disappointing for Sharon and her husband, Todd, is that their "pumpkin-pine" kitchen floor, which they had professionally refinished, has behaved more like an old pumpkin than an old floor, and is on the verge of rotting away.

"When we bought the house in 2003, the floors were pretty messed up, but you couldn't really tell because the previous owner had left so much stuff in the house," Sharon said. "I could see enough of the floor to decide that I'd have to have them refinished right away. The house was built in the 1840s, but other than the pumpkin-pine kitchen floor, the flooring is not original. The oak flooring on the first floor, for example, was nailed to the original floor of pine. The second floor has a mix of woods and includes oak. All the boards are random width, but they don't look old enough to be original."

Sharon and Todd hired a refinishing company—actually a couple of teachers who do the work part-time for extra money—to redo the first floor, the stairs to the second floor (oak was used for stairs in the 19th and 20th centuries because it held up well to heavy traffic), the second-floor hallway, and two bedrooms. The refinishers gave a different price for each room, but it worked out to about $4 per square foot for sanding, staining, and two coats of polyurethane—a standard price for professional refinishing. The job involved about 800 square feet of flooring in the 1,500-square-foot townhouse.

One bedroom floor had a dark stain and "was marked up so badly that Todd didn't think anything could be done about it," Sharon recalls. "Because

The typical wood floor can be refinished up to three times, and at the rate of about once every 15 years. Too much sanding thins the flooring, weakening it and reducing its capability of holding new stain.

buying the house had left us tight on money, he wasn't sure that we should spend $3,000 to have the floors refinished anyway. But now, both he and I are glad we did because, except for the pumpkin-pine kitchen floor that we should have replaced, the floors look absolutely wonderful. The refinishers warned us about the kitchen floor because it is such a soft wood, and we will have to replace it soon. I'm not sure what we will replace it with. I considered tile, but now I'm thinking about laminate because it would continue the wood look from the front of the house to the back."

The job, which was completed before Sharon and Todd moved in, took slightly more than a week, slowed by the arrival of damp, warm weather that reduced drying time of the stain and the polyurethane. The refinishers, who kindly offered color suggestions and stained some boards so the couple could choose, sanded lightly between each coat. They covered the forced-air heating registers to prevent sawdust from falling into the furnace, but left dust removal on the walls until all the sanding was done (baseboards and molding were removed to let them sand to the walls). Some of the boards were cracked and had pieces missing and the refinishers used wood filler to correct the problems.

"The walls have a textured finish, and three years later, I'm still removing dust in the crevices of the finish," Sharon said.

After the floors were refinished, Sharon and Todd bought area rugs for most of the rooms to protect the new finish, and installed a runner on the stairs and matching carpeting on the second-floor hallway.

"I wish the floors had been carpeted when we bought the house," Sharon said. "At least carpeting would have offered some protection to the wood floors underneath."

Sometimes what is under the carpet is better off being out of sight.

Index